GCSE Physics

Volume 2

Energy, Heat, Light and Sound

Dr Asad Altimeemy

Preface

This book is the second volume of three books on GCSE Physics. As stated in Volume 1, the books are designed to help the highest performing students achieve Grade 7 or above. This book is the result of teaching Physics for last 23 years. I have always supported my students with extensive typed notes and fully worked answers and exemplars. I have used these detailed notes to create a comprehensive study aid, which includes notes and fully answered questions. These notes will help you check and consolidate your learning. The book covers all the requirements for most exam boards. However, I have added and extended some topics which I consider are very important for a fuller understanding of essential topics to achieve Grades 8 or 9. To achieve the higher grades, you should make thorough notes and answer all the questions independently. The book has more than 88 fully answered examples and questions to enable you to master these grades. Questions which have the * symbol are Grade 9 questions.

Dr Asad Altimeemy

B.Sc., Ph.D., P.G.C.E, M.Inst.P.

December 2018

CONTENTS

CHAPTER 1

Energy Resources

Energy

Energy is defined as: Energy enables physical work to be done. Further details are explored in 'Work done' discussed in volume 1, Forces and Motion.

Energy may exist in a variety of forms and may be transformed from one type of energy to another. However, these energy transformations are constrained by a fundamental principle, the Conservation of Energy principle which states that energy cannot be created or destroyed.

The unit of energy is joule or J. One joule is the amount of energy required to lift 0.1 kg mass from the surface of earth to 1 m height.

Forms of energy:

Chemical, nuclear, electrical, heat, light, sound, potential (gravitational and elastic) and kinetic energy.

The sources of energy are:

Solar, Wind, Tidal, Waves, Geothermal, Nuclear, Biomass and Fossil fuels like Coal, Oil and Gas

Power Stations

Power stations convert an energy resource into electrical energy. The energy resources may be non-renewable, such as fossil fuels or nuclear power, or renewable, such as hydroelectric, tidal, wave, wind, solar, geothermal and biomass.

Non-renewable energy is an energy which comes from sources that will run out or will not be replenished in an average human lifetime or even in many, many lifetimes. Renewable energy is energy which is naturally replenished on an average human lifetime.

Fossil fuels, nuclear power, geothermal energy and biomass are all used to boil water and to make steam which turns a turbine.

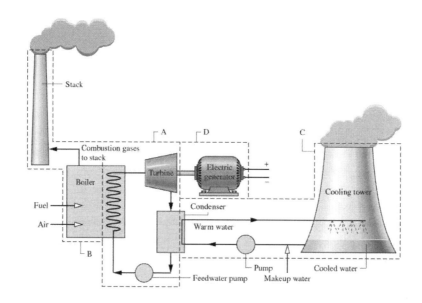

The rotating turbine is connected to a generator which produces alternating current electricity. This electricity is then put through a step-up transformer and transmitted across the National Grid. Electricity, generators and transformers is covered in Volume 3.

Fossil Fuels

Most of the electricity generated in the world today comes from power stations which burn fossil fuels.

Fossil fuels are coal, oil and natural gas. The original source of the energy is the Sun. Plants use sunlight energy for photosynthesis. Coal is made from plant remains. Oil and natural gas are made from both plant and animal remains, which in turn, received their energy from eating plants.

Advantages of fossil fuels

1. They give a large amount of energy from a small amount of fuel.
2. They are readily available. If you need more energy, you just burn more fuel.
3. They are relatively cheap.

Disadvantages

1. They are non-renewable. Once you burn them, they are gone.
2. They cause pollution. Burning a fossil fuel can produce carbon dioxide, sulphur dioxide and smoke. Carbon dioxide is a greenhouse gas and causes global warming. Sulphur dioxide causes acid rain.

3. Power stations use water as a coolant and may return warm water into a river. This decreases the amount of dissolved oxygen in the river.

Nuclear Power.

Nuclear power stations use the heat generated by fission of a fuel (either uranium or plutonium) to boil water to make steam. The steam is used to turn a turbine. Nuclear Physics is covered in Volume 3.

Advantages of Nuclear Power.

1. A large amount of energy is generated from a very small amount of fuel.
2. The fuel is readily available. If you need more energy, you just use more fuel.
3. Nuclear Power does not produce carbon dioxide and so does not contribute to global warming or acid rain.

Disadvantages.

1. Poisonous waste is produced, some of which is highly radioactive. Disposal of this radioactive waste has not been safely achieved. Very long half-lives (thousands of years) mean that the waste will be a danger "forever". At present, the most dangerous waste is sealed in glass-like blocks which are buried deep within "stable" rocks. Careless disposal of waste in the past has led to pollution of land, rivers and the ocean.
2. A power station is very expensive to build and to safely dismantle afterwards (called decommissioning). When the costs are considered, the electricity produced by the power station is relatively expensive.

Hydroelectric Power.

A large river which falls down a steep slope is suitable for generating hydroelectric power. The river is dammed at the top and the valley is flooded, creating a large reservoir (lake) of water. The water is let out through turbines at the bottom of the dam. The turbines turn a generator which produces electricity. The original source of the energy is the Sun which makes the wind blow and the rain fall. Gravity causes the falling water to turn the turbines.

Advantages of hydroelectric power.

1. It is renewable.
2. It is readily available. If you need more energy, you just let out more water through the turbines.
3. It does not cause pollution.

Disadvantages.

Flooding the river valley will destroy the local habitat for many of the species which live there.

Tidal Power

A dam (barrage) is built across an estuary. The barrage has turbines in it. When the tide comes in, water flows through the turbines generating electricity. The water can be stored behind the barrage and then released out through the turbines as the tide goes out, again generating electricity. The original source of the energy is the gravitational pull of the Moon and Sun as they pull the sea backwards and forwards, creating tides.

Advantages

1. It is renewable.
2. It is reliable. The tide goes in and out twice a day.
3. It does not cause pollution.

Disadvantages.

1. It may not look as nice as the unspoiled river.
2. Boats may not be able to get past the barrage.

Wave Power

Wave power uses the rise and fall of the sea as waves approach the coast.
A float on the water surface pushes air forwards and backwards through a turbine on the land, as the waves cause the float to rise and fall. The turbine generates electricity. The original source of the energy is the Sun which makes the wind blow causing waves.

Advantages of wave power.

1. It is renewable.
2. It does not cause pollution.

Disadvantages.

1. It is unreliable. When the wind drops, the waves get smaller and less electricity is generated.
2. An individual wave power machine produces a small amount of electricity. You would need a lot of them to replace one fossil fuel power station.
3. The natural beauty of an area may be spoiled.

Solar Power.

Solar energy is a clean, renewable energy resource that is very useful where energy is needed in remote locations.

There are several ways that we have harnessed the Sun's rays to use this energy resource:

- Photovoltaic Cells
- When light is incident on some materials, an electric current begins to flow. Photovoltaic cells use the photoelectric effect to generate electricity.
- Solar Heat Collectors
- Solar thermal concentrating systems use either mirrors or lenses to concentrate the Sun's rays to produce very high temperatures.

Advantages

1. It is renewable.
2. It does not cause pollution.

Disadvantages.

1. It does not work well when the sky is cloudy (less Sun). It is does not work at night (no Sun).
2. It is relatively expensive. Solar cells produce electricity more expensively than any other source except non-rechargeable batteries.

Geothermal Power.

Some countries have hot underground rocks close to the Earth's surface. Water is pumped down to the rocks through a pipeline and returns to the surface as steam through another pipe. The steam is then forced through a turbine which turns a generator. The original source of the energy is radioactive decay of unstable nuclei within the Earth.

Advantages

1. It is renewable.
2. It is reliable.
3. It does not cause pollution.

Disadvantages.

It is limited to being used in those parts of the world where hot rocks are near the surface.

Biomass - Wood burning.

A wood burning power station is similar to one which burns fossil fuel. The original source of the energy is the Sun. Growing trees use sunlight energy for photosynthesis.

<u>Advantages of wood burning.</u>

1. It is renewable. Trees can be grown at the same rate as they are burnt.
2. It is reliable.
3. Although burning wood produces carbon dioxide, it does not contribute to global warming. This is because the growing trees take in carbon dioxide for photosynthesis at the same rate that the power station emits carbon dioxide during burning.

<u>Disadvantages.</u>
1. Wood burning produces sulphur dioxide which causes acid rain.
2. A large area is needed to grow enough trees to keep the power station running. The land could be used for other purposes, for example growing food.

Wind Power
The wind is caused by the Sun's energy setting up convection currents in the Earth's atmosphere.

<u>Advantages:</u>
1. It is renewable.
2. The running costs when set-up are cheap.
3. There is no air pollution.

<u>Disadvantages.</u>

1. It is unreliable as it is not always windy.
2. It is expensive to set-up.
3. It is a diluted source of energy.
4. It is unsightly and noisy.
5. Only a few areas are suitable.

Energy Transfer and Efficiency
Energy can be transformed from one to another or transferred from one place to another. Energy cannot be created or destroyed.

The thing which transfers energy from one form into another is called a device. Below are some examples of energy transfers of various devices.

An engine will transfer some of the available chemical energy into rotational energy and some into heat. We can calculate the efficiency of the engine using the equation

$$efficiency(\%) = \frac{\textbf{useful energy out}}{\textbf{total energy in}} \times 100\%$$

$$efficiency(\%) = \frac{\textbf{useful power out}}{\textbf{total power in}} \times 100\%$$

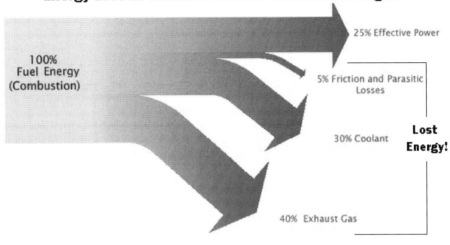

$$efficiency(\%) = \frac{\textbf{25}}{\textbf{100}} \times 100\% = 25\%$$

The engine wastes 75% of energy only 25% is useful.

Examples

1. (a) Coal, gas, oil and wood are all examples of fuels.

(i) What are fuels?

Sources of energy

(ii) Write the names of these fuels in the table below to show which are renewable and which are non-renewable.

Renewable Fuels	Non renewable Fuels
Wood	Coal
	gas

	oil

(b) The list below shows energy resources which are not fuels.

Geothermal, nuclear, solar, tides, wind

Write the names of the energy resources in the table below to show which are renewable and which are non-renewable.

Renewable Energy	Non renewable Energy
geothermal	nuclear
solar	
tides	
wind	

(c) Why is it better to use more renewable energy resources rather than non-renewable resources?

The supplies of non renewable source of energy are limited and eventually will depleted.

Most non-renewable energy source produces pollution and green house gases.

2. The diagram below shows four stages in the production of electricity by a coal-fired power station.

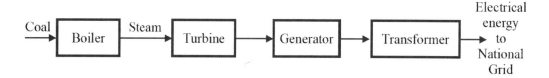

(i) Write down two environmental problems which are caused by burning coal to generate electricity.

Green houses gases, pollution and Acid rain

(ii) How may these environmental problems be reduced?

Removal of exhaust gases, use alternative source not producing CO_2

While nuclear energy has it own pollution problems. Nuclear energy is cleaner source of energy compare to coal, it does not produce greenhouse gases

(b) Some data for a power station is given below.

Maximum continuous power rating of a generator 500 MW at 23 500 V

Energy content of coal used 2.66×10^{10} J per tonne. Total quantity of coal used each day 18 289 tonnes

Use the given data to calculate:

(i) the total electrical energy output each day.

$$Energy = Power \times time$$

$$= 500 \times 10^6 \times 3600 \times 24 = 4.32 \times 10^{13}\, J/day$$

(ii) the total input of coal energy each day.

Input Energy = $2.66 \times 10^{10} \times 18289 = 4.86 \times 10^{14}$ J/day

(iii)the efficiency of the power station.

$$efficiency = \frac{Energy\ out}{Energy\ In} \times 100\% = \frac{4.32 \times 10^{13}}{4.86 \times 10^{14}} \times 100\% = 8.88\,\%$$

(c) Energy is conserved.

(i) Choose one of the stages in the diagram at the start of the question. State what happens to the wasted energy during this stage.

Boiler, heat is lost to surroundings

Turbine, not all steam energy used. Heat and sound lost to surroundings

Generator, heat in wires of the coils of the generator. Heat is lost to surroundings

Transformer, heat in wires of the coils of the transformer, heat to surroundings

(ii) Explain what happens to all wasted energy during energy transfers.

Energy spread out and diluted, energy lost as heat difficult to use for further useful energy transfers

3. In a power station energy is used to generate electricity.

(a) Name three fuels which are commonly burnt in power stations to produce this energy.

Coal, Gas and Oil

(b) Electrical energy can be produced using wind power.

(i) Describe two advantages of using wind power compared to burning fuels.

Renewable and clean energy resource, it does not produce any pollution of greenhouse gases.

(ii) Describe two disadvantages of using wind power compared to burning fuels.

Amount of energy is variable. It depends on wind speed.

CHAPTER 2

Thermal Physics

Heat and Temperature

Heat is related to temperature, but the two are not the same. Imagine that you have a bucket full of water and a cup full of water both at 25 °C. If you add the same amount of heat energy (for example 20,000J) to both, you would find that the temperature of the cup of water increases by much more than the temperature of the bucket of water. If you double the mass, you must double the heat energy to heat it to the same temperature.

Temperature is a measure of the kinetic energy of the particles (how fast they are going). Temperature does not depend on the mass of the substance. The amount of heat energy which a substance has depends on its mass.

Based on kinetic theory, internal energy is the total kinetic energy and potential energy of all the molecules that make up a system. Pressure is a result of collisions between molecules and the container walls. Molecules are in continuous random motion. The average kinetic energy of the molecules is proportional to the absolute temperature of the gas.

Temperature is measured with a thermometer. There are many types of thermometer, but each makes use of a thermometric property (i.e. a property whose value changes with temperature) of a thermometric substance.

For example: mercury in glass thermometer makes use of the change in length of a column of mercury confined in a capillary tube of uniform bore; a platinum resistance thermometer makes use of the increase in the electrical resistance of platinum with increasing temperature.

To establish a temperature a scale, it is necessary to make use of fixed points.

A fixed point is the single temperature at which it can be expected that a physical event (e.g. the melting of ice under specific conditions) always takes place. Three such points are defined below.

- The ice point is the temperature at which pure ice can exist in equilibrium with water at standard atmospheric pressure, 273.15 K.

- The steam point is the temperature at which pure water can exist in equilibrium with its vapour at standard atmospheric pressure, 373.15 K.

- The triple point of water is that unique temperature at which pure ice, pure water and pure water vapour can exist together in equilibrium, 273.16 K.

Thermodynamic scale

The thermodynamic scale is the one that is used for scientific measurement. It is totally independent of the properties of any substance. It is, therefore, an absolute scale of temperature.

It is measured in units called kelvins (K). This scale is defined using one fixed point, the triple point of water. 0 K or -273 °C is absolute zero, it is the lowest limit for the thermodynamic temperature scale, nothing can be colder.

Celsius scale

The Celsius scale is now defined by $\theta = T - 273.15$.

Where T is the temperature in kelvin

Solid, Liquid and Gas

Any substance may exist as solid, liquid or gas. If a solid is heated, it will melt to become a liquid. The temperature at which it melts is called its melting point. If the liquid is then cooled, it will freeze. The temperature at which it freezes is called its freezing point. The melting point and the freezing point is the same for the same substance.

Similarly, if a liquid is heated it will boil to become a gas. The temperature at which it boils is called its boiling point. If the gas is then cooled, it will condense to become a liquid again. A gas will condense at its boiling point.

Sometimes a heated solid will turn into a gas without becoming a liquid. This is called sublimation. Examples of solids which sublime are iodine and carbon dioxide.

The state of a substance (whether it is solid, liquid or gas) depends on its temperature.

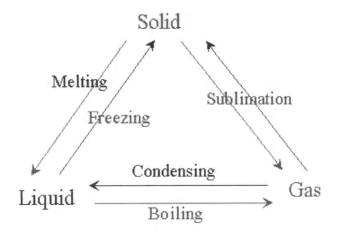

Solid

In a solid, the particles are arranged in a regular pattern. They are close together. They have strong forces holding them in place. They can vibrate but cannot move around. This explains why solids are usually hard materials with a definite shape.

As the solid is heated, the particles vibrate more and more until the force of attraction between them is overcome. Above this temperature, the solid has become a liquid.

Liquid

A liquid has an arrangement of particles which are close together, but they are free to move because the force of attraction between the particles is weaker than it is in a solid. A liquid will flow to take the shape of its container. Its volume is fixed. It cannot be compressed because the particles are already close together.

As the liquid is heated, the particles move faster and faster until they overcome the force of attraction between them. Above this temperature, the liquid has become a gas.

Gas

The particles are not arranged in any pattern. They are about 10 times further apart than in solids and liquids. The forces between them are very weak. They are free to move around and fill any space available. This explains why gases have no fixed shape and can be easily compressed.

The speed at which the particles move depends on the temperature. The higher the temperature, the faster the movement.

In a gas, the particles move fast in random directions. There is no force of attraction between the particles. It is said to have short range order which means that the arrangement only repeats itself for a small number of particles.

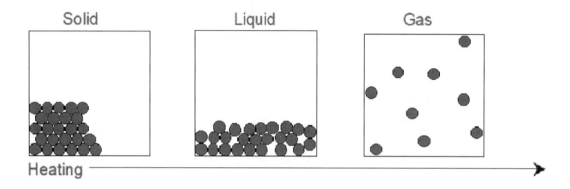

Change of state (Melting and boiling)

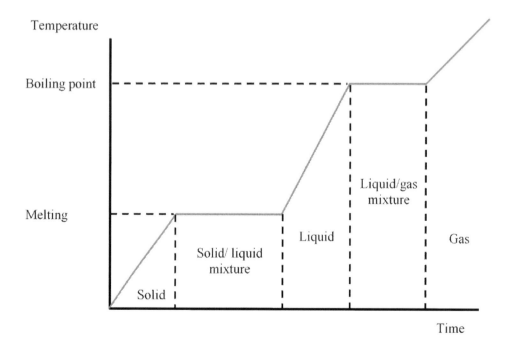

The graph above, shows the change in temperature of a substance as it is heated steadily. It starts off as a solid, melts and finally boils.

Expansion of solid, liquids and gases

As a solid is heated, the molecules vibrate more violently and the solid expands in all directions. For a simplicity, we only going to consider the expansion in length.

Different materials expand by different amounts for the same rise in temperature. The expansion of materials most be considered for in the construction of buildings and bridges where large steel girders are used and where very great stresses develop.

The amount of expansion depends on: material, length or volume and temperature rise.

For a change in length this can be expressed as:

$$Change\ in\ length\ =\ \alpha \times original\ length\ \times temperature\ change$$

where α is the linear expansivity of the material, defined as the fractional change in length for a unit rise in temperature or:

$$\alpha\ =\ \frac{L - L_o}{\theta L_o}$$

where L_o is the original length L the final length and the change in temperature.

The bi-metallic strip

This is a strip of two different metals welded together, one side is brass (high expansion) the other is iron (low expansion). When the strip is heated it bends with the brass always on the outside of the curve. The bi-metallic strip is a useful device for detecting and measuring temperature changes.

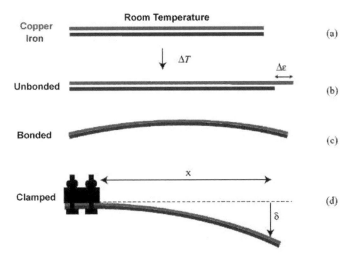

The expansion of liquids

All liquids expand more than all solids. The volume of the liquid gets greater as it is heated. The greater the rise in temperature, the more it expands. The actual change in shape of the liquid depends on the shape of the container that it is in.

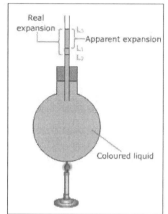

In the experiment with the coloured water in a glass flask, if you watch very carefully, you will see the level of the water go down when you first start heating. This is because the glass gets hot first and so expands and the volume of the beaker therefore increases. This means that the water level will drop. Then the water starts getting hotter, it expands more than the glass and so the water level rises.

The expansion of the liquid which we observe is called the apparent expansion. The real expansion of liquid is greater than the observed apparent expansion.

This is because of the expansion of the liquid's container which takes up some of the liquid's expansion.

One important use of this is in the liquid in glass thermometer. Mercury is often used in thermometers. But for low temperatures, alcohol is preferred because it freezes at a lower temperature.

In a thermometer, the expansion of the liquid is "magnified" by allowing liquid to expand up a very narrow tube. A small increase in volume will large change the liquid level in the tube.

Freezing

When liquid freezes, the molecules become bonded together. They are still moving but instead of being free to move anywhere, they can now only vibrate. They are now a solid.

The volume of the solid is usually smaller than the liquid from which it was formed. However, water is different, its volume increases when it freezes. This strange behaviour is very important. As ice has a greater volume than water, it is less dense than the water and so it floats. This means that ponds freeze from the top downwards.

At 4°C, water has its greatest density and so it will sink to the bottom of the pond. The water above will be colder until just below the ice it is at 0°C.

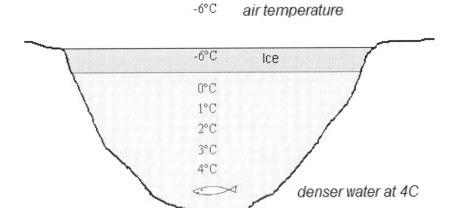

Expansion of gases

When a gas is heated, the molecules in the gas move round faster. The more it is heated, the faster they move and the hotter the gas becomes. If it can, the volume of the container increases. There is also another effect, because the molecules are hitting the walls of the container faster, they cause a greater force on the container and so the pressure of the gas in the container rises.

Heat capacity and specific heat capacity

The amount of heat energy needed to change the temperature of a substance depends on:

(a) what the substance is;
(b) how much of it is being heated;
(c) what rise in temperature occurs.

The heat energy needed to raise the temperature of an object by 1 K is called the heat capacity of an object.

The specific heat capacity of a substance is the heat needed to raise the temperature of 1 kg of the substance by 1K (or by 1°C).

The units for Specific heat capacity are J/(kg K) or J/(kg°C).

Substances with high specific heat capacities take a lot of heat energy and therefore a long time to heat up and a long time to cool down.

Heat energy = mass × specific heat capacity × temperature change

$$E = m \times c \times \theta$$

where m is mass, c is the specific heat capacity and θ is the change in temperature.

Examples

4. How much heat energy is needed to raise the temperature of 3 kg of copper by 6 K?

(Specific heat capacity of copper = 385 J/(kg K)

Heat energy = mass x specific heat capacity x temperature change

$$= 3 \times 385 \times 6 = 6930J$$

5. What is the rise in temperature of 5 kg of water if it is given 84 000 J of heat energy?

Specific heat capacity of water = 4200 J/(kg ^oC).

$$E = m \times c \times \theta$$

$$\theta = \frac{E}{m \times c} = \frac{84000}{5 \times 4200} = 4\,°C$$

6. If 48 000 J of heat energy are given off when a 2 kg block of metal cools by 12⁰C, what is the specific heat capacity of the metal?

$$E = m \times c \times \theta$$

$E = 2 \times 48000 \times 12 = 1152000\ J$

7. Water has a high specific heat. Why is this useful when it is used as a coolant in engines?

Water will absorb large amount of energy for small increase in temperature.

Latent heat

When a substance changes its state from a solid to liquid or from a liquid to a gas heat energy is needed. This energy is used not to heat up the substance but to separate the molecules from each other. This energy is called Latent Heat energy. The units for specific latent heat are joules/kilogram (J/kg).

While a solid is melting and while a liquid is boiling, there is no temperature change. The temperature only changes when the change of state is complete.

The amount of heat needed to change the state of 1 kg of a substance is called the Specific Latent Heat of the substance. It can take a different amount of heat to change the solid into a liquid than to change the liquid into a gas and so a substance will have two specific latent heats.

The specific latent heat of fusion is the heat needed to turn 1 kg of solid into a liquid at its melting point. The specific latent heat of vaporisation is the heat needed to turn 1 kg of liquid into a gas at its boiling point.

Heat energy to melt or boil something = mass × specific latent heat

$$E = m \times l_v$$

where m is mass and l_v is the latent heat for vaporisation

$$E = m \times l_f$$

where m is mass and l_f is the latent heat for fusion (solid to liquid)

When a gas condenses and when a liquid freezes latent heat is given out. The amount of heat that was used to melt or boil the substance is released. When steam at 100^0C condenses to water, it gives out a lot of heat and we can use this fact to explain why a scald from steam at 100°C is much more painful than a scald from water at the same temperature.

Examples

8. Find the energy needed to change 4 kg of water at 100°C into steam at 100°C.

Specific latent heat of vaporisation of water = 2 260 000 J/kg.

Energy required = 4 × 2 260 000 = 9 040 000 J.

*9. Find the energy needed to change 900 g of ice at 0°C to water at 5°C. Specific latent heat of fusion of water = 334 000 J/kg and specific heat capacity = 4200 J/kg K

In this question ice at 0 °C absorbs energy to converts to water at 0 °C and then water at 0 °C to absorb more energy to heat water to 5 °C.

Energy required to convert ice to water =m × l_f=0.9 × 334000 = 300600 J.

Energy required to heat water to 5 °C = m×c×θ = 0.9 × 4200 × 5 = 18900 J

Total energy = 300600 + 18900 = 319500 J

10. a)   How much energy is needed to turn 5 kg of water, at 100^0C into steam at 100^0C? Specific latent heat of vaporisation of water = 2 300 000 J/kg.

Energy = m × l_v = 5×2300000= 11500000 J

b) What is meant by

(i) specific latent heat of fusion?

The amount of heat energy required to change 1 kg of substance from solid to liquid.

(ii) specific latent heat of vaporisation?

The amount of heat energy required to change 1 kg of substance from liquid to vapour.

*11. How much heat energy is given out when 1500 g of steam at 100^0C condense and cool to 50^0C? Specific latent heat of vaporisation of water = 2 300 000 J/kg and Specific heat capacity of water = 4200 J/kg ^oC

Energy released from steam at 100 ^oC condensing water at 100 = m × l_v = 1.5 × 2300000 = 3450000 J

Energy released from cooling water at 100 ^oC to water at 50 ^oC = m×c×θ = 1.5 × 4200 × (100-50) = 315000 J

Total energy = 3450000 + 315000 = 3765000 J

Heat Transfer
Heat is transferred naturally from a substance with a higher temperature to a substance with a lower temperature.

Heat can be transferred in three ways:

1. Conduction - by a substance which does not move (solids).
2. Convection - by a substance which moves (liquids and gasses).

3. Radiation - infra-red radiation is exchanged between all substances.

Conduction

Heat can be transferred by conduction only in solids. If one end of a solid is heated, the particles of the solid gain kinetic energy. This means that, they move faster.

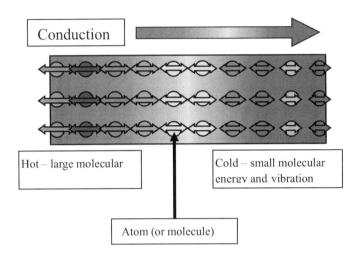

Conduction

Hot – large molecular

Cold – small molecular energy and vibration

Atom (or molecule)

In a solid, the particles are held together by strong forces of attraction. The only way in which the particles can move is to vibrate forwards and backwards or vibrational motion.

When the solid is heated, the amount by which the particles vibrate is increased. The increase in energy is passed on to the next particle through collisions with the next particle, which in turn starts to vibrate more and collide with next one.

In non-metals, the process is slow. It takes a long time for the particles to pass on their heat. Non-metals are not good conductors. They are good insulators.

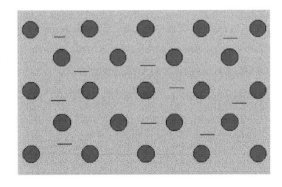

Metals conduct heat quickly. Metals have atoms which are surrounded by delocalise electrons or free electrons. These free electrons can travel quickly and easily throughout the structure. The electrons transfer the heat energy by colliding with other atoms and electrons in the metal.

Air as an insulator

Air is such a bad conductor that we often use it to help keep things warm. Layers of clothing have air pockets in them to keep our bodies warm in cold weather. For the same reason, birds fluff up their feathers in winter.

The cavity walls in houses are often filled with foam to stop the air from moving about and dragging in cold air from outside. The space between the roof and the ceiling is called the loft. Glass fibre is laid across the loft to reduce heat transfer out of the roof. The glass fibre with trapped air is a very poor conductor which reduces heat transfer from the ceiling to the loft. Conduction is very poor because both the polymer and the trapped air are good insulators.

Double Glazing

Double glazing involves two layers of glass with a small air gap between them. It works as an insulator in much the same way as cavity wall and loft insulation. The air gap is too small to allow the air to circulate. This prevents heat transfer by convection. The trapped air is a very poor conductor which reduces heat loss through the window.

Convection

Heat can be transferred by convection in liquids and gases. When a liquid or gas is heated, it will expand and increase in volume. Therefore, it become less dense. The warmer gas or liquid will rise, and colder gas or liquid will replace it. The process will repeat itself again when the colder gas or liquid is heated.

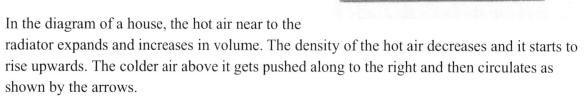

We can define convection currents as the flow of liquid or gas caused by change in density; the whole medium moves and carries heat energy with it. The liquid or gas which transfers the heat can circulate around and around between the hot and cold regions.

In the diagram of a house, the hot air near to the radiator expands and increases in volume. The density of the hot air decreases and it starts to rise upwards. The colder air above it gets pushed along to the right and then circulates as shown by the arrows.

The arrows show the convection currents. As the hot air moves around the room, it loses its heat by collision with the walls, ceiling and the objects in the room.
Finally, the colder air circulates near to the radiator, where it is heated and the whole process

repeats itself.

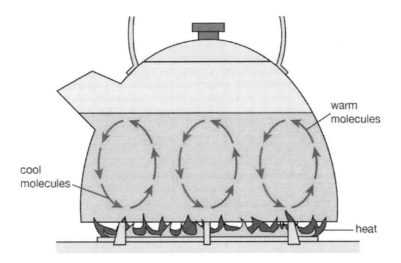

Land and sea breezes

At places on the coast in summer-time, it is noticeable that a breeze generally blows in from the sea during the day, while at night the direction of the wind is reversed. These breezes are local convection currents. During the day, the land is heated by the sun to a higher temperature than the sea.

Land has small specific heat capacity compared to the sea. During daytime, the land heats up quickly, the air above it rises, and cool air is drawn in from the sea, sea breeze. At night time, the land cools quickly while the sea stays warm. Air rises above the sea and a breeze blows off the coast onto the sea.

Radiation

Radiant heat consists of invisible electromagnetic waves which can pass through a vacuum (Infa-red radiation). These waves are partly reflected and partly absorbed by objects on which they fall. The part which is absorbed becomes converted into heat. Radiant heat which has passed through a vacuum can be easily felt by holding the hand near to a vacuum-filled electric lamp when the current is switched on. A more general discussion on the subject of electromagnetic waves will be found the next chapter.

Infra-red radiation transfers heat between all objects. Infra-red radiation is an electromagnetic wave and can travel through a vacuum.

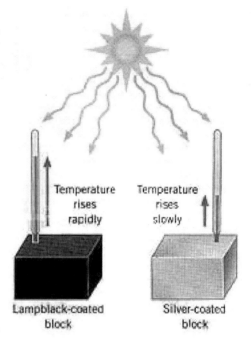

Heat from the Sun reaches us through the vacuum of space by travelling as visible light. Objects absorb the light and reradiate it as infrared radiation. An object can absorb, emit and reflect radiation. A hot object will emit more infra-red radiation than it absorbs. A cold object will absorb more infra-red radiation than it emits. In this way heat is transferred from hotter to colder objects. An object whose temperature does not change will emit infra-red radiation at the same rate as it is absorbed.

Objects which are at the same temperature as each other will absorb, emit and reflect infra-red radiation at different rates depending on the type of surface which the object has.

An object with a matt (dull) surface will absorb and emit infra-red radiation at a faster rate than an object with a shiny surface. An object with a dark surface will absorb and emit infra-red radiation at a faster rate than an object with a light surface.

Heat leaves the metal more quickly through the matt black surface than the shiny white surface.

When an infra-red radiation falls on an object, some will be reflected, and some will be absorbed. The greater the proportion of radiation which is reflected, the less will be absorbed.

An object with a matt or dark surface will be a poor reflector of infra-red radiation. An object with a shiny or light surface will be a good reflector of infra-red radiation. Shiny metal foil can be placed behind a radiator in a room to increase its efficiency. The foil reflects radiation back into the room which heats the air rather than heating the wall. This adds to the efficiency of convection in the room.

The Vacuum Flask

The vacuum flask has several ways of keeping the heat in or out. The shiny surfaces prevent heat radiation and reflect any heat energy that falls on them.

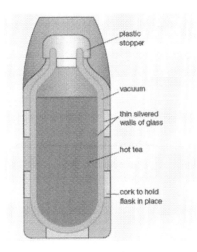

The partial vacuum between the two sides of the flask reduces conduction to a very small amount and the stopper prevents heat loss by convection.

Greenhouse

Visible light, short-wave radiation, from the Sun, can pass through the glass; this then warms up the things inside the greenhouse and they emit much longer wavelength heat radiation. It is this longer wavelength radiation from warm objects that cannot get through the glass and so the inside of the greenhouse warms up. The glass of the greenhouse also prevents convection currents carrying the warmed air out of the greenhouse. Opening the roof vents in a greenhouse will prevent it heating up too much.

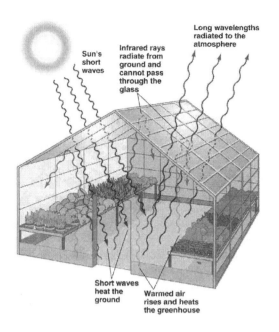

Evaporation

The molecules in a liquid are in a state of continuous motion, some moving faster than others. In the middle of the liquid, they collide with each other. But at the surface of the liquid, some of them are going fast enough to escape from the liquid.

The molecules need energy to escape and so the hotter the liquid becomes, the more evaporation there is.

During evaporation, the more energetic particles escape from the surface, leaving the less energetic particles behind. Therefore, the average kinetic energy of the particles in liquid will decrease, causing the temperature of the liquid to decease.

Evaporation is very important in the cooling of surfaces of objects. If we put a drop of methylated spirit on your hand, the methylated spirit will evaporate and your hand will feel cold. The molecules of methylated spirit get the energy they need from your hand, leaving the molecules of the hand with less energy and so it becomes colder. The same thing happens when you sweat, only in this case you are losing water from your body by evaporation.

Heat Sink

A heat sink is an object that absorbs and dissipates heat from another object, using thermal contact.

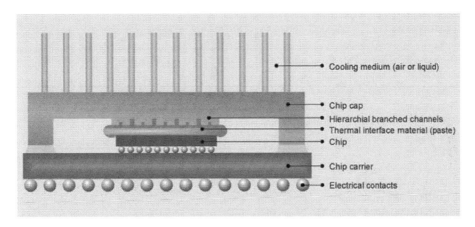

'Cooling fins' are projections that increase the surface area from which heat can be radiated away from a device. The fins project outwards, making the area for emitting heat back, into, say, an electronic circuit's container, smaller than the area emitting heat to the outside environment. This means that the heat energy is efficiently transferred outside the device's housing. Fins are found on a motorbike engine. They have a very large surface area to let heat out to the surroundings, as quickly as possible.

Example

12. (a) The diagram shows a hot water system.

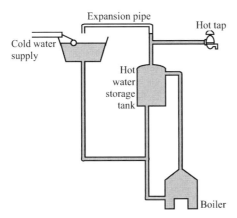

(i) Explain why the boiler is below the hot water tank.

Hot water expands, it become less dense and rise.

(ii) Why is heat energy transferred from hot water in the tank to the surrounding air?

Convection heat

inside the tank is hotter than outside.

(iii) Name the process by which energy is transferred through the sides of the tank.

conduction

(iv) How may heat loss from the hot water tank be reduced?

Insulate the tank to reduce heat is lost to the surround. Using trapped air in fibre glass to insulate the tank.

(b) One way of reducing heat loss from a house is by cavity wall insulation. Foam is pumped between the inner and outer brick walls as shown in the diagram.

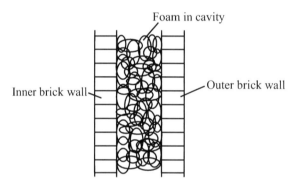

How is heat loss from a house reduced by:

(i) having a cavity wall?

air is a good insulator

(ii) convection stopped

The foam is using trapped air an insulator. As the air is trapped, there will be no convection.

13. The diagram shows a section through a gas oven.

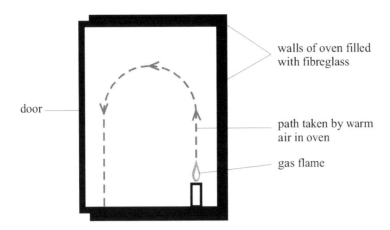

walls of oven filled with fibreglass

door

path taken by warm air in oven

gas flame

Use words from the list to complete the sentences.

conduction   convection   insulation   radiation   resistance

The outside of the door gets hot because energy is transferred through

the door by ….conduction

Energy is transferred from the gas flame to the rest of the oven by the movement of air.

This type of energy transfer is called ......Convection...

The walls of the oven are packed with fibreglass to reduce energy transfer. Energy transfer

is reduced because fibreglass provides good …..insulator

The outside of the cooker is white and shiny.

This reduces energy transfer by ….radiation

14.   The drawing shows water being heated in a metal saucepan.

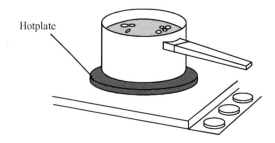

Hotplate

(a)   Explain, in terms of the particles in the metal, how heat energy is transferred through the base of the saucepan.

Electrons and molecules gain energy from the hot plat. Molecules will vibrate faster with a larger amplitude collide with molecules near to it. Through the collision and vibration heat will transfer through the base. Electrons transfer energy through the base.

 (b)   Energy is transferred through the water by convection currents. Explain what happens to cause a convection current in the water. The answer has been started for you.

   As heat energy is transferred through the saucepan, the water particles at the bottom

   Hot water will expand and become less dense. As the density of the hot water is less than the density of cold water, hot water will rise

(c)   Some energy is transferred from the hotplate to the air by *thermal radiation.* What is meant by *thermal radiation*?

   Transfer of energy by waves, infrared radiation

15.   The diagram comes from a leaflet about a "coal effect" gas fire.
It shows how air circulates through the fire.

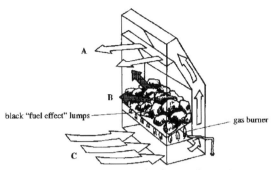

(a) Explain in detail why the air travels from **C** to **A**.

Convection current. Air is heated by the burner, air particles gain energy, air expand and becomes less dense, air hot rises. Hot air moves from C to A

(b) The black "fuel effect" lumps become very hot.

    (i) Name the process by which the lumps transfer thermal energy to the room as shown at **B**.

        radiation

    (ii) Suggest **one** feature of the black "fuel effect" lumps which make them efficient at transferring energy.

        Black surface is very good emitted to thermal radiation. large surface area will improve the efficiency.

16. The vacuum flask shown has five features labelled, each one designed to reduce beat transfer.

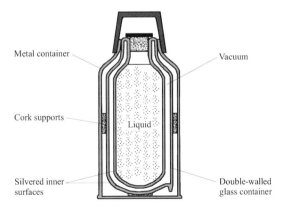

(a) (i) Which labelled feature of the vacuum flask reduces heat transfer by both conduction and convection?

Vacuum

(ii) Explain how this feature reduces heat transfer by **both** conduction and convection.

Conduction and convection require particles. In particles in a vacuum.

(b) (i)Which labelled feature of the vacuum flask reduces beat transfer by radiation?

Silvered surface

(ii) Explain how this feature reduces heat transfer by radiation.

Silvered surface is poor emitter to radiation.

17.   (a)   The diagram shows part of a solar water heater. Water circulating through the solar panel is heated by the Sun.

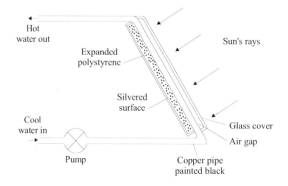

(i)   Complete the following sentence.

Heat energy is transferred from the Sun to the solar panel by

Radiation

(ii)   The pipe inside the solar panel is black. Why?

Good absorber to heat radiation

(iii) There is a layer of expanded polystyrene behind the black pipe. Why?

Reduce heat loss from the panel.

(iv)   A silvered surface is used at the back of the solar panel. Explain why.

To reflect heat radiation back into the panel

18. (a) The diagram shows two ways to reduce heat loss through the walls of a house.

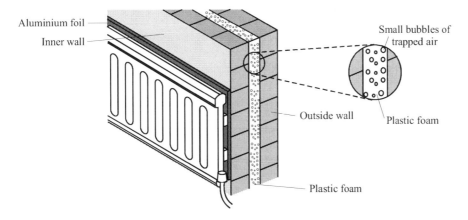

(i)   How is the aluminium foil able to reduce heat loss?

reflects heat back into the room

(ii)   The plastic foam is good at reducing heat loss through the walls. Explain why.

Trapped air is a good insulator

(d) Evaporation is an important heat transfer process. When sweat evaporates, it takes heat energy from your body. As humidity increases, you are more likely to feel hot and uncomfortable. Explain why.

The rate of evaporation decreases, less heat energy removed from the body.

19. **(a)** A shiny metal can and a dull black can are filled with the same amounts of cold water. A radiant heater is placed exactly half way between the cans as shown in the diagram below.

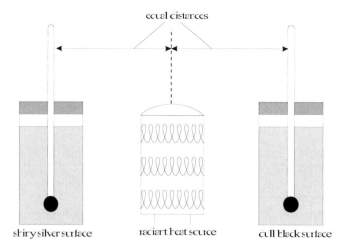

equal distances

shiny silver surface   radiant heat source   dull black surface

Two thermometers are used to measure the temperature of the water in each can every minute.

(i)   Suggest how the temperature of the water in the dull can would be different from the temperature of the water in the shiny can after ten minutes.

Rise more quickly

(ii)   Explain your answer to part (i).
Dull surface good absorber to heat radiation

(b)   The radiant heater was removed and both the cans were filled with the same amount of boiling water, as shown in the diagram below.

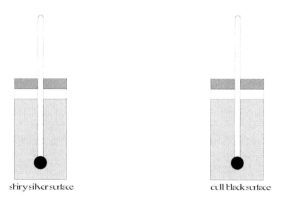

shiny silver surface   dull black surface

The temperature was recorded every minute for ten minutes.

(i)   Suggest how the temperature of the water in the dull can would be different from the temperature of the water in the shiny can after ten minutes.

(ii)

Fall more quickly

(ii)   Explain your answer to part (i).

Dull surface good emitter heat radiation

House Insulation

Heat energy is transferred from homes by conduction through the walls, floor, roof and windows.

It is also transferred from homes by convection. For example, cold air can enter the house through gaps in doors and windows, and convection currents can transfer heat energy in the loft to the roof tiles. Heat energy also leaves the house by radiation through the walls, roof and windows.

Ways to reduce heat loss

There are some simple ways to reduce heat loss, including fitting carpets, curtains and draught excluders. Heat loss through windows can be reduced using double glazing. There may be air or a vacuum between the two panes of glass. Air is a poor conductor of heat, while a vacuum can only transfer heat energy by radiation.

Heat loss through walls can be reduced using cavity wall insulation. This involves blowing insulating material into the gap between the brick and the inside wall, which reduces the heat loss by conduction. The material also prevents air circulating inside the cavity, therefore reducing heat loss by convection.

Heat loss through the roof can be reduced by laying loft insulation. This works in a similar way to cavity wall insulation.

U values

It is useful for architects to know the rate of loss of heat per square metre through a material when the difference of temperature across its faces is 1K. This will also depend on the thickness of the specimen, so the values given below can only be regarded as approximate.

The U-value measures how well a building component, e.g. a wall, roof or a window, keeps heat inside a building. For those living in a warm climate the U-value is also relevant as it is an indicator of how long the inside of the building can be kept cold. In both cold and warm climates good U-values are important measures for understanding the amount of energy that is needed to keep a comfortable inside temperature.

$$U = \frac{Power}{area \times Temperature\ difference}$$

Example

20. The diagram below shows a house which has not been insulated. The cost of the energy lost from different parts of the house for one year is shown on the diagram.

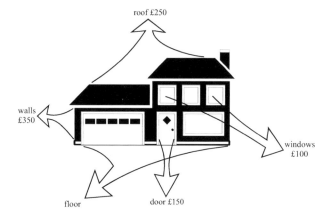

(a) The total cost of the energy lost during one year is £1000.

(i) What is the cost of the energy lost through the floor?

1000-250-100-150-350 = £150

(ii) Suggest one way of reducing this loss.

floor covering or Insulation under floor

(b) The table below shows how some parts of the house may be insulated to reduce energy losses. The cost of each method of insulation is also given.

WHERE LOST	COST OF ENERGY LOST PER YEAR (£)	METOD OF INSULATION	COST OF INSULATION (£)
roof	250	fibre-glass in loft	300

walls	350	foam filled cavity	800
windows	100	double glazing	4500
doors	150	draught proofing	5

(i) Which method of insulation would you install first? Explain why.

Draught proof doors or fibre glass in loft or in cavity. It is very low cost and it is easy to install

(ii) Which method of insulation would you install last? Explain why.

Double glazing as it costs most and it saves least energy.

Work done by a gas during expansion

Consider an ideal gas at a pressure P enclosed in a cylinder of cross- sectional area A.

The gas is then compressed by pushing the piston in a distance dx, the volume of the gas decreasing by dV. We assume that the change in volume is small so that the pressure remains almost constant at P (isobaric process).

Work done on the gas during this compression $= F \times \Delta x$

Pressure $= F/A$ and $\Delta V = A \times \Delta x$

$$Work\ done \ = \ \frac{F}{A}\ A\ \Delta x \ = \ Pressure \ \times \ Volume$$

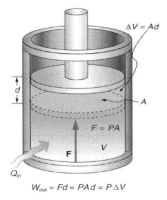

The Work done equation is also applies when a gas is compressed, in which case work is being done *on* the gas. Doing work on a gas increases the internal energy of the gas and can cause an increase in the temperature of the gas.

The Work done equation can be applied only if the change takes place reversibly. If it does not, the values of pressure and temperature at any instant will be different in different regions of the gas.

CHAPTER 3

THE GAS LAWS

Boyle's Law

At constant temperature T, the pressure of a fixed mass of gas is inversely proportional to its volume.

Pressure (P) × volume (V) = constant

A graph of pressure against volume is shown in the following diagram for three different temperatures T_1, T_2 and T_3 ($T_1 > T_2 > T_3$). The lines on it are isothermals.

If a fixed mass of gas with a pressure P_1 and a volume V_1 changes at constant temperature to a pressure P_2 and volume V_2, Boyle's Law can be written as:

$$P_1V_1 = P_2V_2$$

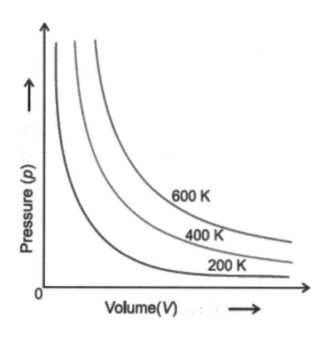

Charles' Law

At constant pressure (P), the volume (V) of a fixed mass of gas at constant pressure is directly proportional to its absolute (in kelvin) temperature (T)

The equation for the line was first suggested by the French Physicist Jacques Charles in 1787.

It states that for an ideal gas:

Volume (V) = constant × absolute temperature (T)

$$\frac{\textbf{\textit{Volume of the gas}}}{\textbf{\textit{Temperature of the gas}}} = \textbf{\textit{constant}}$$

$$\frac{V}{T} = c$$

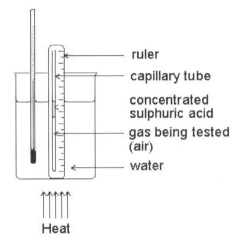

If the gas is heated so that its volume changes from volume 1 to volume 2 while its temperature changes from temperature 1 to temperature 2 then:

$$\frac{Volume1}{Temperature1} = \frac{Volume2}{Temperatur2}$$

$$\frac{V_1}{T_1} = \frac{V_2}{T_2}$$

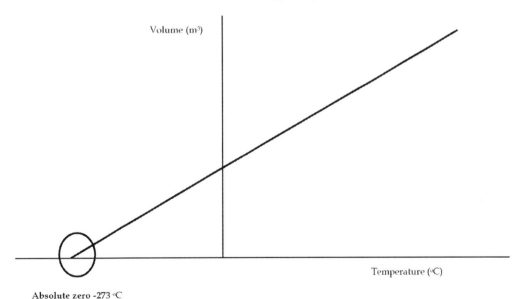

The Pressure Law

The pressure (p) of a fixed mass of gas at constant volume is directly proportional to its absolute temperature (T)

Variation of the pressure with temperature

Pressure (P) = constant × absolute temperature (T)

If a fixed mass of gas with a pressure P_1 and a temperature T_1 changes to a pressure P_2 and temperature T_2 with no change of volume, this can be written as:

Pressure law for a gas:

$$\frac{P_1}{T_1} = \frac{P_2}{T_2}$$

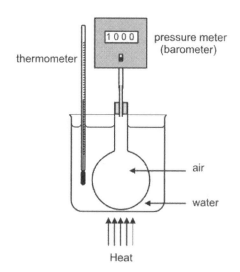

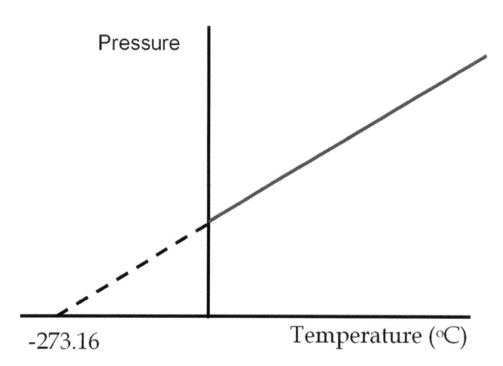

Ideal gas

An ideal gas is a theoretical gas which has the following properties:

- A gas consists of a large number of identical molecules.
- molecules behave as if they were hard, smooth, elastic spheres
- Intermolecular collisions and those between molecules and the container walls are perfectly elastic (i.e. there is no loss of kinetic energy)
- molecules are in continuous random motion;
- the average kinetic energy of the molecules is proportional to the absolute temperature of the gas;
- the molecules do not exert any noticeable attraction on each other. (It cannot be liquify)
- the volume of the molecules is infinitesimal when compared with the volume of the gas
- the time spent in collisions is small compared with the time between collisions.

Air at atmospheric pressure and room temperature behaves like an ideal gas. The use of ideal gas simplifies many equations.

Ideal gas equation

$PV = constant,$

$\frac{P}{T} = constant$ and

$\frac{V}{T} = constant$

gives:

$\frac{PV}{T} = constant$

If we use 1 mole of gas, the constant is known as the molar gas constant (R). So for one mole of the ideal gas equation is:

Ideal Gas equation (one mole): $PV = RT$

$$PV = nRT$$

Where n is number of moles

Examples

21. 0.3 m³ of an ideal gas are heated at constant pressure from 27° C to 127° C. What is the new volume of the gas? Remember to convert all temperature to K.

$$V2 = [V1T2]/T1 = [0.3 \times 400]/300 = 0.4 \; m^3$$

Now the volume of one mole of an ideal gas at Standard Temperature and Pressure (STP) (1.014×10^5 Pa and 273.15 K) is 0.0224m³ and so

$$1.014 \times 10^5 \times 0.0224 = 1 \times R \times 273.15 \qquad \text{and therefore R} = 8.314 \; \text{JK}^{-1}\text{mol}^{-1}.$$

For n moles this equation becomes:

Ideal Gas equation (n moles): $PV = nRT$

For a change from P_1, V_1 and T_1 to P_2, V_2 and T_2 the equation can be written:

$$\frac{P_1 V_1}{T_1} = \frac{P_2 V_2}{T_2}$$

One mole is the amount of substance which contains the same number of elementary units (atoms or molecules) as there are atoms in 12 grams of carbon 12 (^{12}C)

The number of atoms in 12g of carbon-12, which is equal to the number of elementary units per mole, is called the Avogadro number N_A.

$N_A = 6.02 \times 10^{23}$ mol^{-1}

The relative molecular mass (M_r) of a substance is defined by:

$$M_r = \frac{mass \; of \; a \; molecules \; of \; the \; substance}{mass \; of \; the \; carbon - 12 \; atoms} \times 12$$

The molar mass (M_m) of a substance is the mass per mole of the substance.

$M_m = M_r$ (in gram) $= M_r \times 10^{-3}$ (in kg)

Number of moles $n = \dfrac{M}{M_m}$

M is the mass of the substance.

$$n = \frac{N}{N_A}$$

where N is the number of molecules

22. A petrol - air mixture in the piston of a car engine initially has a volume of 50cm^3, a temperature of 27° C and is at a pressure of 2×10^5 Pa. When it is ignited by the spark plug, the volume increases to 450cm^3, and the pressure drops to 8×10^4 Pa. What is the final temperature of the mixture? (Assume that it behaves as an ideal gas!)

$$\frac{P_1 V_1}{T_1} = \frac{P_2 V_2}{T_2}$$

$$\frac{200000 \times 50}{(27 + 273)} = \frac{80000 \times 450}{T_2}$$

$$T_2 = \frac{10800000000}{10000000} = 1080 \, K$$

23. The air in a closed cylinder at a pressure of 50000Pa and at 27°C is heated to 227°C. What is its new pressure?

Change the temperature to kelvin $T_1 = 27 + 273 = 300$ K

T2 = 227 + 273 = 500 K

Using

$$\frac{P_1}{T_1} = \frac{P_2}{T_2}$$

$$\frac{50000}{300} = \frac{P_2}{500}$$

$$P_2 = \frac{50000 \times 500}{300} = 83333.3 \, Pa$$

24. The temperature of the gas in a closed cylinder is reduced to 0.5 of the original value. What happens to its pressure?

$$\frac{P_1}{T_1} = \frac{P_2}{T_2}$$

$$\frac{P_1}{T_1} = \frac{P_2}{0.5T_1}$$

$$P_2 = 0.5\,P_2$$

25. A fixed mass of gas has a volume of 2m³ at 80°C and at a pressure of 150 000Pa. The pressure is now reduced to 100 000Pa and the volume is decreased at the same time to 0.5 m³. What is the final temperature of the gas?

$T_1 = 80 + 273 = 353$ K

Using

$$\frac{P_1 V_1}{T_1} = \frac{P_2 V_2}{T_2}$$

$$\frac{150000 \times 2}{353} = \frac{100000 \times 0.5}{T_2}$$

$T_2 = 58.8$ K

Brownian Motion

In 1827, while using a microscope to study tiny grains of pollen suspended in water, Robert Brown discovered that the grains were constantly wobbling and wandering about. Some years later it was discovered that the Brownian motion is a result of constant collisions between water molecules and grains of pollens.

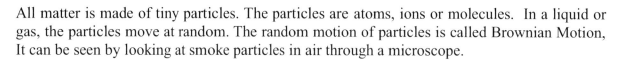

Any minute particle suspended in a liquid or gas moves chaotically under the action of collisions with surrounding molecules.

All matter is made of tiny particles. The particles are atoms, ions or molecules. In a liquid or gas, the particles move at random. The random motion of particles is called Brownian Motion, It can be seen by looking at smoke particles in air through a microscope.

CHAPTER 4

WAVES AND LIGHT

Waves

Waves transmit energy without transmitting matter. This means that waves can move energy from one place to another without moving any material from one place to another. The amount of energy which a wave has depends on its amplitude. Most waves move through material, but only move vibrating the molecules of the substance without moving the molecules with the wave.

After the wave has gone, the molecules of the material are back where it started but energy has been carried by the wave from its origin to its destination.

For example, a fishing float will simply bob up and down as a water wave passes it, the boat does not move along in the direction that the wave is moving.

We could classify waves into two categories based on its motion. Transverse and Longitudinal

Transverse Waves

When a transverse wave travels through a substance, the particles of the substance are moved at right angles to the direction in which the wave is travelling. After the wave has gone, the particles are back where they started.

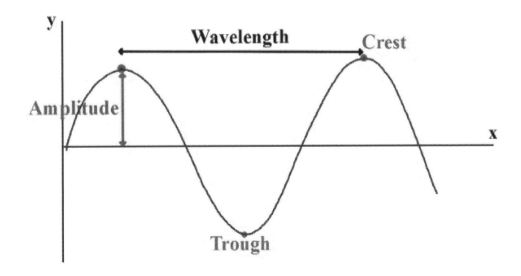

Examples of transverse waves

- Sea waves,
- Electromagnetic waves.

Longitudinal Waves

When a longitudinal wave moves through a material, the particles of the material move backwards and forwards along the direction in which the wave is travelling.

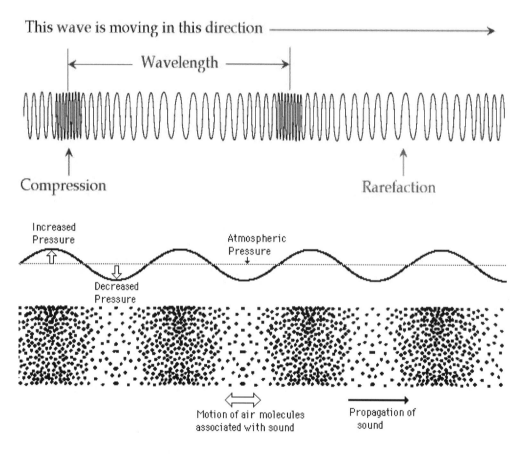

The wavelength can be measured as the distance between the centres of two compressions.

Examples of longitudinal waves are:

- Sound
- Primary waves from earthquakes.

Properties of Waves

The amplitude of the wave is measured from the peak (or trough) to the mid-point. Amplitude can be defined as "the maximum displacement from the average position". Amplitude is a measure of how much energy the wave has.

Wavelength, λ, is the distance between two peaks or the distance between two troughs. Wavelength can be defined as "the distance the wave has travelled during one complete cycle". The unit of wavelength is metres

Period (T) of a wave is the time taken for a particle of the medium through which the wave travels to make one complete oscillation. The unit of period is second.

Frequency (f) is the number of complete waves passing a given point per second. The bigger the frequency the higher the pitch of the note or the bluer the light. The unit of frequency is hertz, Hz.

1 Hertz = 1 cycle per second.

The period = 1 ÷ frequency.

Speed how fast the wave transfers energy from one place to another. This is about 330 m/s for sound in air and a massive 300 000 000 m/s for light in space.

$$Speed = \frac{distance}{time}$$

If the distance travelled by the wave equals to its wavelength, then the time taken equals to the period.

$$Speed = \frac{\lambda}{T} = \lambda \times f$$

$$speed = Frequency \times Wavelength \qquad v = f \times \lambda$$

Intensity is the power per unit area at that point.

$$I = \frac{P}{A}$$

Where I is the intensity, P is power and A is the area

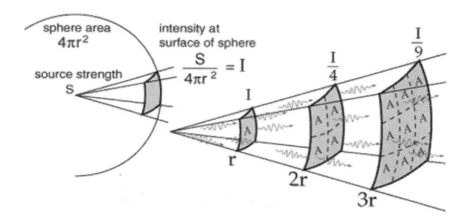

Reflection

Reflection best occurs from flat, hard surfaces. For light a flat shiny surface, like a plane mirror, is a good reflector. A plane mirror is one which is straight and not curved.

The light ray which hits the mirror is called the incident ray. The light ray which bounces off the mirror is called the reflected ray.

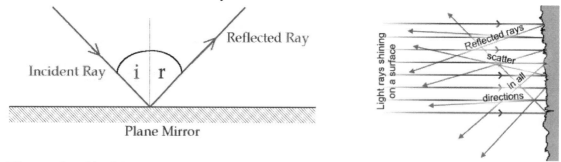

The angle of incidence equals the angle of reflection, i = r.

This means that whatever angle the light ray hits the mirror, it will be reflected off at the same angle. If the surface of the mirror is not smooth but rough or bumpy, then light will be reflected at many different angles. The image in the mirror will be blurred and unclear. This is called diffuse reflection.

When you look into a mirror, you see a reflection, which is the image of the real object.

The image appears to be the same distance behind the mirror as the real object is in front of

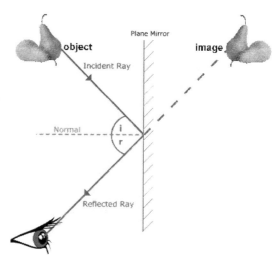

it. This is because the brain thinks that light travels in straight lines without changing direction.

The image is called virtual because it does not really exist behind the mirror.
Laws of reflection

1. The angle of incidence is equal to the angle of reflection.
2. The incident ray, the reflected ray and the normal all lie in the same plane.

Waves Reflection

Any type of wave can be reflected. Note that the line representing the wave front or peak.

After reflection, a wave has the same speed, frequency and wavelength; it is only the direction of the wave that has changed.

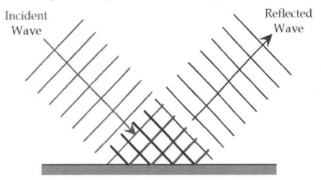

Refraction

Any type of wave can be refracted, which means a change of direction.
Refraction can occur when the speed of a wave changes, as it moves from one medium to another.

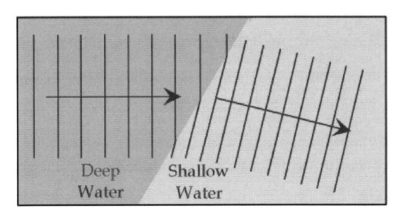

After refraction, the wave has the same frequency but a different speed, wavelength and direction. When a wave enters a new medium, its change in speed will also change its wavelength

If the wave enters the new medium at any angle other than normal to the boundary, then the change in the wave's speed will also change its direction.

Light travels at different speeds in different materials because they have different densities. The higher the density, the slower light travels. Light travels fastest in space (a vacuum) and a little slower in air.

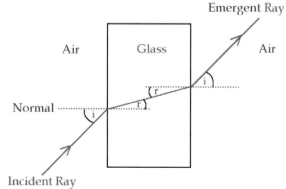

A line drawn at right angles to the boundary between the two media (air and glass) is called a normal.

Light which enters a glass block along a normal does not change direction, but it does travel more slowly through the glass and so its wavelength is smaller.

In going from a less dense medium (air) to a denser medium (glass) light bends towards the normal.

This means that i > r (the angle i is greater than the angle r).

In going from a denser to a less dense medium (glass to air), light bends away from the normal.

How much the light bends depends on its colour or frequency.

The change in angle of the light ray is the same when it enters and leaves the glass. If the incident ray had continued without changing direction, then the emergent ray would be parallel to it.

Laws of refraction
1. The incident ray, refracted ray and the normal all lie in the same plane.

2. The ratio

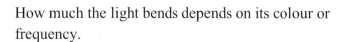

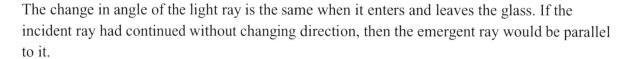

Snell's Law

The amount refraction of light depends on a property of the material known as its refractive index. This property connects the angle of incidence (i) with the angle of refraction (r).

$$Refractive\ index = \frac{\sin i}{\sin r} = \frac{n_2}{n_1} ----(1)$$

Where n_1 is the refractive index of medium1 and n_2 is the refractive index of medium 2.

For a light beam travelling from medium 1 to medium 2, the relative refractive index $_1n_2$ is found by using the following formula:

$$1n2 = \frac{n_2}{n_1} ;\quad 1n2 = \frac{\sin i}{\sin r}$$

from equation 1

$$n1 \sin i = n2 \sin r \quad and \quad \frac{n2}{n1} = \frac{c1}{c2}$$

$$Therefore:\ c2 \sin i = c1 \sin r$$

The greater the refractive index, the more the light refracts. Glass has a refractive index of 1.5, water 1.3 and diamond 2.42. This means that light will bend more when it hits a diamond than it will when it hits a piece of glass of the same shape. It is partly this that makes diamonds sparkle so much.

Example

26. A ray of light hits a glass block which has a refractive index of 1.5 at an angle of incidence of 30°. Calculate the angle of refraction.

sin i/ sin r = 1.5 = sin 30/sin r

therefore

sin r = 0.33   r = 19.6 °

Total internal reflection and critical angle

When a light ray emerges from glass, high refractive index, into air, low refractive index, it is refracted and bends away from the normal, so i < r. As i is made bigger, the refracted ray gets closer and closer to the surface of the glass.

When i equals the critical angle, the refracted ray is just touching the glass surface.

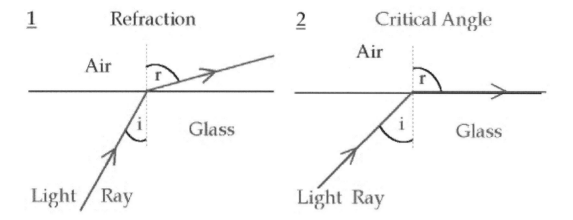

The critical angle is different for different combinations of materials. The critical angle for glass and air is different than glass and water. Total internal reflection happens when angle of incidence is bigger than the critical angle.

When a light ray tries to move from glass to air at an angle greater than the critical angle, the refracted ray cannot escape from the glass. Refraction cannot happen, therefore, all of the light is reflected at the glass / air boundary, as if it had hit a mirror, i = r.

Total Internal Reflection

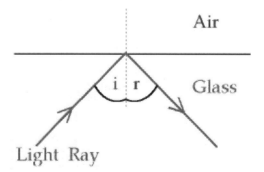

It is called internal reflection because it occurs inside the glass, and total because all the light must be reflected.

From the above, we can summarise that for a total internal reflection to occur, light has to travel from high optical density medium to low density medium and the angle of incident is greater than the critical angle.

For light travelling at the critical angle

$_2n_1 = \sin i / \sin r = \sin c / \sin 90 = 1/_1n_2$

For light passing from a material of absolute refractive index n_1 to one of absolute refractive index n_2 we have:

Critical angle (θ_c):

$$\sin \theta_c = \frac{n_2}{n_1}$$

For $n_2 = 1$, i.e air this becomes: $n_1 \sin \theta_c = 1$

$$\sin \theta_c = \frac{1}{n}$$

For an air-glass boundary, with n = 1.5, c = 42° and for an air-water boundary c = 48.5°

Total internal reflection explains the shiny appearance of the water surface of a swimming pool when viewed at an angle from below. The phenomenon is used in prismatic binoculars (Mirages are caused by continuous internal reflection.)

Optical Fibres

An optical fibre is a long thin strand of glass which has an outer plastic coating. Light from a laser enters at one end of the fibre, striking the surface of the glass at an angle greater than the critical angle.

Total internal reflection occurs at the glass surface and the light cannot escape until it reaches the other end of the fibre. The plastic coating prevents the glass surface from getting scratched, which might allow the light to escape through the side of the fibre.

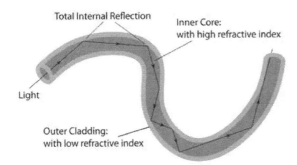

Optical fibres are used in endoscopes and for telecommunications.

Real and apparent depth

The refraction of light at the surface of water makes ponds and swimming pools appear shallower than they really are. A 1m deep pond would only appear to be 0.75 m deep when viewed from directly above.

There is a connection between the real and apparent depths of the water. It can be proved that:

$$Refractive\ index = \frac{real\ depth}{apparent\ depath}$$

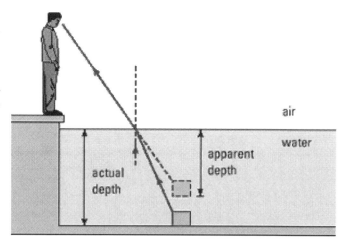

The mirage

Mirages are usually associated with hot deserts. The traveller in a desert often sees what appears to be a sheet of water a short distance ahead of him. This he is never able to reach, since it is an optical illusion.

To understand a mirage, you must first understand how temperature affects the path light takes. If light travels through constant temperature, then it will travel in a straight line. However, cold air has a higher index of refraction than hot air does. This is since cold air is more dense than hot air and light travels slower through it.

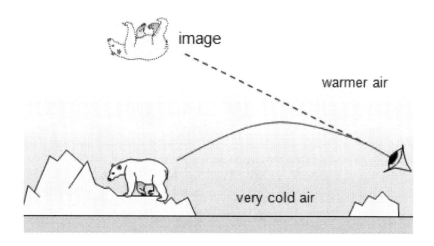

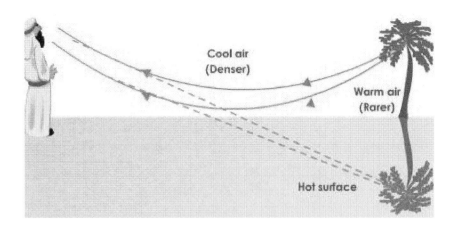

Dispersion

If a beam of light of one colour is shone through a prism, the direction of the beam is changed by the prism.

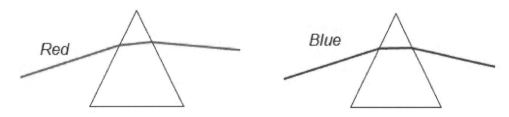

Red light refracts less than blue light. If a white light is used, the prism splits up the light into a series of colours.

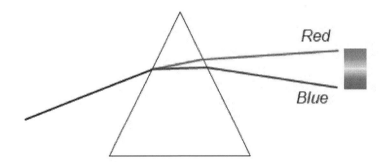

The dispersion of white light into a spectrum occurs because the different colours are refracted by different amounts by the glass of the prism. Red light is refracted the least. Violet is refracted the most.

Violet light is refracted most by a prism and red light is refracted least.

The source of light may also emit infra-red and ultraviolet light. Infra-red light is heat radiation with a longer wavelength than red light. A thermometer placed at IR will show a rise in temperature. Ultraviolet light has a shorter wavelength than violet light. A fluorescent material will glow when placed at UV.

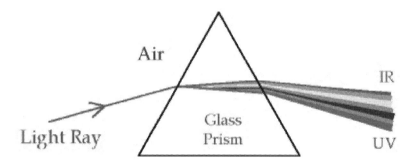

A pure spectrum can be produced by adding two lenses to focus each colour to a point on the screen. If this is not done the colours will overlap.

Examples

27. Calculate the angle of refraction for the following cases:

(a) Angle of incidence 40° in air travelling into water, refractive index 1.33

(b) Angle of incidence 40° in air travelling into diamond, refractive index 2.42

a)

$$1.33 \ = \ \frac{sin \ i}{sin \ r} \ = \ \frac{sin \ 40}{sin \ r}$$

$$sin \ r \ = \ \frac{sin \ 40}{1.33} \ = \ 0.483$$

r = 28,9°

b)

$$2.42 \ = \ \frac{sin \ 40}{sin \ r}$$

$$sin \ r \ = \ \frac{sin \ 40}{2.42} \ = \ 0.265$$

r = 15,4°

28. Define refractive index and explain briefly a method of measuring its value for water.

A penny lies at the bottom of a tank containing water to a depth of 16 cm. Calculate the apparent depth of water. The refractive index of water is 1.33.

Refractive index of a medium is the ration between the speed of the light in vacuum to speed of light in medium.

$$Refractive\ index = \frac{real\ depth}{apparent\ depath}$$

$$1.33 = \frac{16}{apparent\ depath}$$

Apparent depth = 12 cm

29. What is meant by the critical angle of a medium?

The critical angle is angle at which the angle of refraction is 90°.

Show by a ray diagram how a right-angled glass prism may be used: (i) to turn a ray through 90°; (ii) to turn a ray through 180°; (iii) to invert a beam of light.

i)

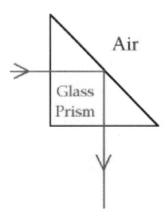

ii)

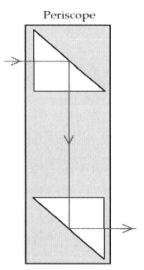

Periscope

iii)

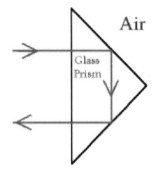

Air

Glass
Prism

30. What happens to the speed of light as it passes from air into a material with a higher refractive index?

The speed of light will decrease.

31. What happens to the wavelength of light as it passes from air into a material with a higher refractive index?

The wavelength will decrease.

Interference

When two groups of waves (called wave trains) meet and overlap, they interfere with each other. The resulting amplitude will depend on the amplitudes of both the waves at that point. Where the waves meet, they are superposed.

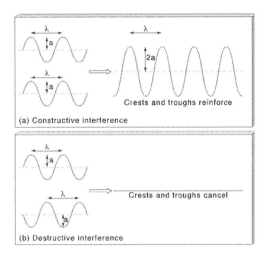

The principle of superposition

At a point where two or more waves meet, the instantaneous displacement is the vector sum of the individual displacement due to each wave at that point.

If the crest of one wave meets the crest of the other, the waves are said to be in phase and the resulting intensity will be large. This is known as constructive interference. If the crest of one wave meets the trough of the other (and the waves are of equal amplitude) they are said to be out of phase by π then the resulting intensity will be zero. This is known as destructive interference.

Diffraction

Diffraction is the apparent bending of waves around small obstacles and the spreading out of waves past small openings.

*Diffraction occurs as a result of the superposition of secondary wavelets from a continuous section of wave front that has been limited by an aperture or the opaque object. Maximum diffraction occurs when the gap size equals the wavelength.

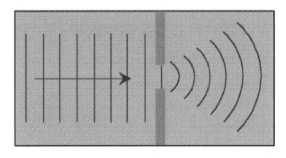

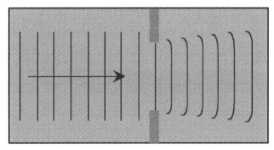

CHAPTER 5

Electromagnetic Waves

Electromagnetic waves are transverse waves which have both an electric and a magnetic effect.

Electromagnetic waves are sometimes called rays or radiation (these words are also used for radioactivity).

All electromagnetic waves travel at the same speed (in a vacuum). Their speed is 300,000,000 m/s in a vacuum.

$c = f \times \lambda$

Where c is the speed of light

They can have a wide variety of wavelengths and frequencies which form the electromagnetic spectrum.

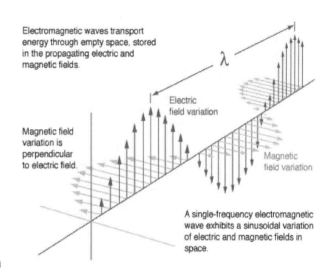

Electromagnetic waves transport energy through empty space, stored in the propagating electric and magnetic fields.

Magnetic field variation is perpendicular to electric field.

Electric field variation

Magnetic field variation

A single-frequency electromagnetic wave exhibits a sinusoidal variation of electric and magnetic fields in space.

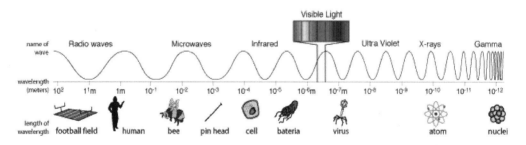

Electromagnetic Spectrum

Electromagnetic waves can have wavelengths which range from several thousand metres to less than one million millionth of a metre. The waves are divided into wavelength ranges according to the wave's effect or uses.

As the wavelength decreases, the frequency increases. Radio waves have the smallest frequency and gamma rays have the largest frequency.

Radio Waves

Radio waves are used for broadcasting radio and TV programmes. The transmitted information may be analogue or digital and uses a radio wave as a carrier.

Microwaves

Microwaves have wavelengths shorter than radio waves. Some of these wavelengths pass easily through the atmosphere and are used to transmit information to satellites. Mobile phone networks use microwaves.

Microwave cookers use microwaves which give energy to the water molecules in food, causing it to get hot. Living cells can also absorb microwaves. The cells may be damaged or killed by the heating effect of the waves.

Infra-red

Infra-red waves are easily absorbed by materials. The energy of the wave causes the material to get hot. We usually think of infra-red radiation as heat. Ordinary ovens, grills and toasters use infra-red radiation to cook food.

Infra-red waves can transmit information through the air to operate different devices by remote control. Information can also be sent through optical fibres. Intense infra-red radiation will damage or kill living cells by burning them.

Ultraviolet

Ultraviolet waves are often called ultraviolet light or ultraviolet radiation.

Some materials will absorb the energy from ultraviolet waves and emit (give out) the energy as visible light. These materials are called fluorescent and are used for fluorescent lighting and security marking.

Ultraviolet light from the Sun causes skin to tan. Sunbeds emit ultraviolet light to give an artificial tan. Intense ultraviolet light in strong sunlight can damage cells which are deep inside skin tissue. This type of damage can result in skin cancer. Darker skin is more resistant to ultraviolet light than lighter skin. Very intense ultraviolet light will kill living cells.

X-rays

Electromagnetic waves with a wavelength shorter than ultraviolet light are called X-rays (not X waves).

X-rays can pass easily through flesh, but not through bone. X-ray photographs are used to show the image of bones against a black background. These photographs can show if bones are broken or damaged. Low intensity X-rays can damage living cells and cause cancer.

People who work with X-rays take measures to protect themselves from exposure. They wear a film badge and stand behind special screens when the X-ray machine is switched on. High intensity X-rays will kill living cells.

Gamma rays

Electromagnetic waves with a wavelength shorter than X-rays are called gamma rays or gamma radiation. Gamma rays may be emitted from radioactive materials.

Low intensity gamma radiation can damage living cells and cause cancer. High intensity gamma radiation will kill cells. It is used in a technique called radiotherapy to treat cancer by targeting the cancer cells with a beam of radiation and then rotating the source of the beam as shown below.

The normal cells receive a lower dose of gamma radiation than the cancer cells, where all the rays meet. Radiotherapy aims to kill the cancer cells while doing as little damage as possible to healthy normal cells.

Gamma radiation is used to kill microorganisms; this is called sterilising. It is used to sterilise food and hospital equipment such as surgical instruments.

Black Body Radiation

This subject is the reason why scientist realised that they need a need type of Physics we called Quantum Physics.

When a substance is heated, it gives out radiation. As it gets hotter and hotter, so the radiation emitted has a shorter and shorter wavelength. There is a spread of wavelengths emitted and most of the radiation that is emitted is at shorter wavelengths, as the temperature rises.

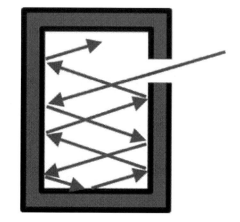

When it gets hot enough, this radiation is so short that it appears as visible light. For many years scientists had struggled to explain the spread of emitted energy with temperature, but without success. They wanted to know why a hot piece of metal glowed first red, then orange, then yellow and finally white as its temperature was increased, why cool stars were red and ones that were hot were bluish white.

A black body is a body which absorbs all the radiation incident on it. A black body radiator is a theoretical object that is totally absorbent to all thermal energy that falls on it, thus it does not reflect any light so appears black.

As it absorbs energy, it heats up and re-radiates the energy as electromagnetic radiation.

Black-body radiation does not depend on the nature of the emitting surface, but it does depend upon its temperature.

At any given temperature, there will be a range of different wavelengths (and hence frequencies) of radiation that are emitted. Some wavelengths will be more intense than others. This variation is shown in the graphs below.

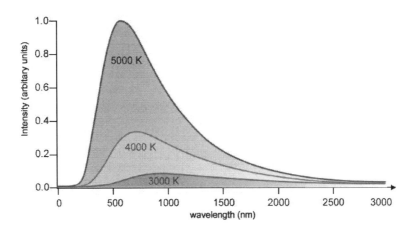

Although stars are not perfect emitters, their radiation spectrum is approximately the same as black-body radiation.

We assume that a star behaves as a perfect 'black body'. In other words, it is a perfect radiator of radiation at its surface temperature.

32. (a) The diagram below shows a ray of sunlight falling on the side of a prism at the point P. A screen is drawn on the other side of the prism. On leaving the prism the sunlight forms a visible spectrum on the screen between the points X and Y.

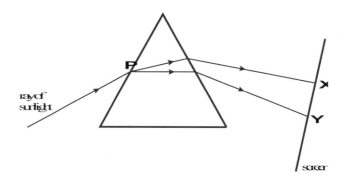

ray of
sunlight

X

Y

screen

(i) Name **one** type of radiation to be found:

   1. above X. Infra-red

   2. below Y. Ultraviolet

(ii) Give **one** use of:

   UV radiation;

   sun tanning

   microwaves.

   Cooking and mobile phone communications

(b) (i) Name a part of the electromagnetic spectrum which is used to sterilise surgical instruments.
   Gamma or X rays

(ii) Explain how this radiation sterilises surgical instruments.

   kills all bacteria

33. Use your ideas about waves to answer the following questions.

   (a) The diagram below shows a boat anchored behind a pier. Sea waves approach the pier from the left.

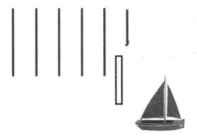

Despite being sheltered by the pier the boat rocks gently up and down.

(i)   Complete the diagram by drawing the waves to the right of the pier.

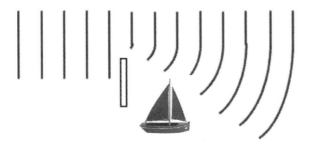

(ii)   What is the name of this process?

Diffraction

(b)   During the course of an experiment a 3 cm radio wave generator was positioned in front of three metal screens as shown in the diagram below.

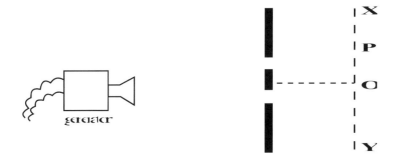

To the right of the screen a radio detector was moved from point **X** to point **Y**, through points **P** and **O**. As it was moved it measured the intensity of the radio waves. It showed that the intensity of the radio waves was high at point **O** and much lower at point **P**.

(i)   Explain why the intensity of the radio waves was high at point **O**.

waves travel the same distance via each gap. Path difference = 0

Constructive interface

(ii)   Explain why the intensity of the radio waves was much lower at point **P**.

Waves travel different distance via each gap. Waves are out of phase, which result in destructive interference

(iii) What is the name of this process?

Interference

34. (a)   The diagram shows wavefronts from a light source approaching a barrier. The waves diffract as they pass through the gap in the barrier.

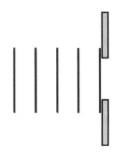

Complete the diagram to show the diffracted wavefronts.

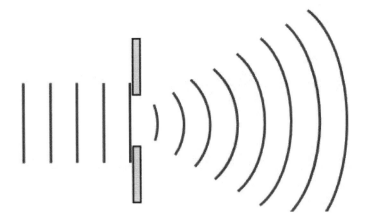

(b)   Wavefronts from a light source refract as the light moves from a dense medium, water, to a less dense medium, air.

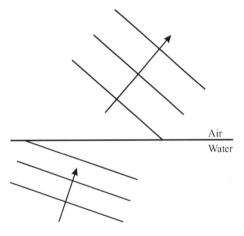

What causes the wavefronts to refract in the direction shown in the diagram?

Refraction

35. In the diagram below A and B are two radio navigation beacons. They both transmit at 1.5 MHz. The waves from both A and B have the same amplitude and they are in phase with each other. A ship is at point X, 1600 m away from each beacon.

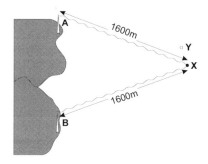

i) Calculate the wavelength of the radio waves.

(The speed of radio waves is 3×10^8 m/s.)

Speed = wavelength × frequency
3.108 = 1.5.10⁶ × wavelength
Wavelength = 200m

ii) Calculate the number of wavelengths which is equal to the distance between A and X.

8

iii) Explain why the ship hears a strong signal.

Waves from X and Y in phase or zero path difference

(iv) As the ship sails from its present position to a point Y the strength of the signal received falls to zero and then builds up again until it is almost as strong as at X.

Explain the changes in signal strength as the ship sails from X to Y. (Y is 1500 m from A and 1700 m from B.)

Moving from X go out of phase till midway of X-Y in antiphase
path difference = wavelength/2 , a destructive interference
then progressively into phase, path difference = wavelength, a constructive interference.

CHAPTER 6

Lenses

A lens is simply a piece of transparent material such as glass, plastic or liquid with one or more curved faces, and the effect that it has on a beam of light depends on the extent and nature of this curvature.

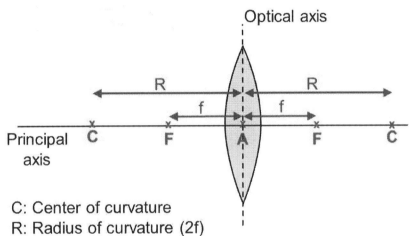

C: Center of curvature
R: Radius of curvature (2f)
F: Focal Point
f: focal length
A: vertex, center of lens

The principal axis of the lens is the line which passes through the centre of curvature of the lens surface.

A principal focus of converging lens is a point to which all rays, incident parallel to the principal axis, converge after refraction by the lens.

A principal focus of diverging lens is a point from which all rays, incident parallel to the principal axis, appear to diverge after refraction by the lens.

Convex lens surfaces have a real and therefore positive radius of curvature. Concave lens surfaces have a virtual and therefore negative radius of curvature. A convex lens has a real and therefore positive focal length. A concave lens has a virtual and therefore negative focal length.

All distances are measured from the pole of the lens and for a thin lens this is almost coincident with the centre of the lens.

The strength of a lens is described in terms of either its focal length or its power. The power of a lens is defined as:

$$Power\ of\ a\ lens\ =\ 1/[focal\ length\ of\ the\ lens\ in\ metres]$$

The unit of power of the lens is m^{-1} or dioptre.

The power of converging lens is positive; that of a diverging lens is negative.

For example, a convex lens with a focal length of 10 cm will have a power of + 10, while a concave lens with a focal length of 5 cm will have a power of -20.

Convex lenses have positive powers while concave lenses have negative powers. The power of a meniscus lens depends on which face of the lens is the more sharply curved.

The effect on a beam of light of a convex lens and concave lens is shown in Figure below. The principal focus (F), focal length (f), centre of curvature (C) and radius of curvature (R) are also shown.

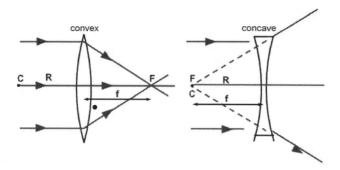

Graphical construction of the image position

The position of an image can be found graphically for a lens using a ray diagram.

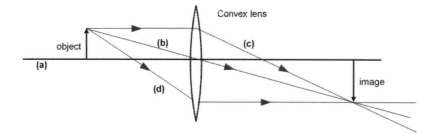

We use three lines to form the image produced by a lens.

(a) the principal axis,

(b) a ray from the top of the object that passes through the centre of the lens (notice that at this point the lens behaves like a parallel-sided block of glass),

(c) a ray from the top of the object, parallel to the axis that goes through the principal focus after passing through the lens

An additional line can be drawn to check the accuracy of the diagram:

(d) a ray from the top of the object through the principal focus that emerges parallel to the axis.

The image of the top of the object is at the point where rays b, c and d cross.

A real image is one through which rays of light pass, and it can therefore be formed on a screen. A virtual image is one from which rays of light only appear to have come from the object, and therefore cannot be formed on a screen. The nature of the image depends on where the object is:

Converging Lens - Image Formation

When the object is at the principal focus (F'), the image is only formed at infinity.

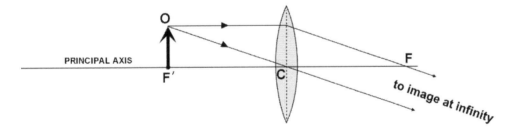

When the object is between the lens and the principal focus (F'), the image is virtual, erect, behind the object and magnified.

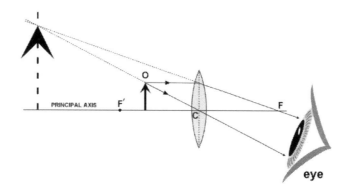

When the object is between the principal focus (F') and 2x the focal distance (2F'), the image is beyond 2F, real, inverted and magnified.

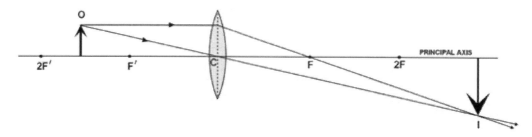

When the object is at 2x the focal length (2F'), the image is formed at 2F, and is real, inverted and the same size as the object.

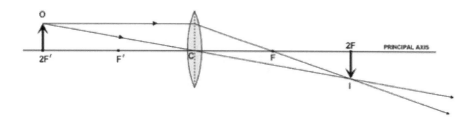

When the object is beyond 2x the focal length (2F'), the image is formed between F and 2F, and is real, inverted and diminished.

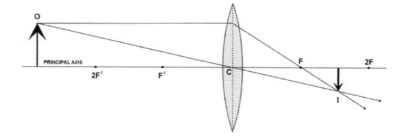

When the object is at infinity, the image is formed at F, and is real, inverted and diminished.

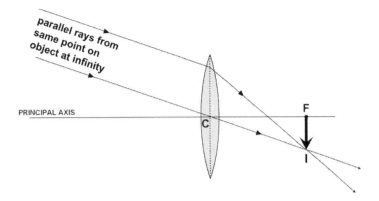

A concave lens forms an upright, virtual image of any object placed in front of it. The image is always smaller than the object and closer to the lens. Changing the position of the object changes the position and size of the image.

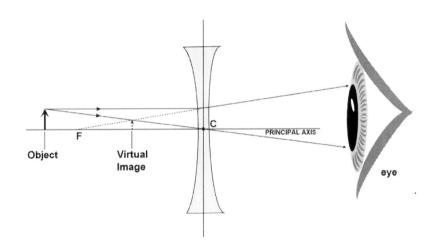

Magnification

The magnification of a lens, like that of a curved mirror, is given by:

$$Magnification\ (m) = \frac{image\ size}{object\ size} = \frac{image\ distance\ (v)}{object\ distance\ (u)}$$

The formula for a thin lens can be shown to be

$$Lens\ formula:\ \ 1/object\ distance\ +\ 1/image\ distance\ =\ 1/focal\ length$$

$$\frac{1}{u} + \frac{1}{v} = \frac{1}{f}$$

This applies to all types of lens as long as the correct sign convention is used when substituting values for the distances. (Reminder: we use the 'real is positive, virtual is negative' sign convention.) u is negative for virtual objects, v is negative for virtual images and f is negative for diverging images

Examples

36. An object 10 mm tall stands vertically on the principal axis of a converging lens of focal length of 10 mm, and at a distance of 17 mm from the lens. Find the position, size and nature of the image.

Using $\quad \dfrac{1}{u} + \dfrac{1}{v} = \dfrac{1}{f}$

$$\dfrac{1}{17} + \dfrac{1}{v} = \dfrac{1}{10}$$

$$\dfrac{1}{v} = \dfrac{1}{10} - \dfrac{1}{17}$$

v = 170/7 = 24 mm

using

$$\dfrac{image\ size}{object\ size} = \dfrac{image\ distance\ (v)}{object\ distance\ (u)}$$

$$\dfrac{image\ size}{10} = \dfrac{24}{17}$$

Image size = 14 mm

The object is real, inverted and magnified

37. Define principal focus, focal length of a converging lens, and explain the meaning of real image and virtual image.

Principal focus of converging lens is a point to which all rays incident parallel to the principal axis converge after refraction by the lens.

Real image is an image made by real rays or rays refracted by the lens.

Virtual image is an image made by virtual rays.

38. A small object is placed 6 cm away from a converging lens of focal length 10 cm. Find the nature, position, and magnification of the image.

Using $\dfrac{1}{u} + \dfrac{1}{v} = \dfrac{1}{f}$

$\dfrac{1}{v} = \dfrac{1}{10} - \dfrac{1}{6}$

v = -60/4 = -15 cm , the image distance is negative, which means it is a virtual image

magnification = 15/6 = 2.5

the image is magnified and erect

Human Eye
Our eyes have several different parts, each of which does different things. The most important parts are:

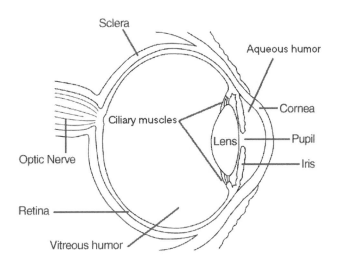

Lens
The lens is a bi-convex converging lens of a jelly-like, flexible and transparent material. The lens has a higher refractive index (n = 1.44) than the surrounding transparent medium (n = 1.33), which maintains the eye's spherical shape. The lens, together with refraction which occurs at the cornea (the front of the eye), forms a real, inverted and diminished image on the retina. The lens is suspended inside the eye by a circular band of ligaments. The ligaments are attached to a circular ring of muscle called the ciliary muscle which controls the shape of the

lens. When the ciliary muscle is relaxed the lens has its longest focal length and focuses rays from distant objects onto the retina. Contraction of the ciliary muscle reduces tension in the lens making it more curved and more powerful. The shorter focal length lens now focuses images of near objects on the retina. Accommodation is the name given to the ability of the lens of the eye to change its focal length and produce focused images of both distant and near objects on the retina.

The eye lens changes its focusing distance by changing its shape. The change in the shape of the lens inside the eye only slightly adjusts the focal length of the whole eye. As the greatest difference in refractive index occurs between the air and the cornea, it is the front of the eye which causes most of the bending of the light rays

Cornea
Cornea – the transparent part at the front of our eye. This helps to focus the view on our retina. Most of the refraction of the light occurs here.

Retina
The retina is the inner layer of the eye which contains light sensitive cells and nerve fibres. Light falling on the retina produces chemical changes in the cells which then send electrical signals along the nerve fibres via the optic nerve to the brain.

The retina contains two types of light sensitive cells which, due to their shapes, are called rods and cones. Over the whole of the retina most of the cells are rods. These are sensitive to a low level of light but do not give much detail or sharpness to the image. At the centre of the retina, at a place called the fovea, cone shaped cells are packed closely together. Around the fovea our eyes have the best detail and colour vision. The point where the millions of nerve fibres leave the retina is a blind spot because it contains no light sensitive cells.

Iris
Iris is this is the coloured part of your eye. If someone has blue eye, it is the iris that is blue. This part of the eye controls how much light gets into your eye. It behaves just like the diaphragm in a camera. In bright light the iris expands so that the hole in the middle of it, the pupil, is small and only lets a small amount of light into your eye. In dim light, the iris contracts so that the pupil gets bigger, allowing more light to get into your eye.

Normal eye
A normal human eye can accommodate the range of distances from about 25 cm (the near point) to infinity (the far point). The near point starts nearer than 25 cm from the eye in young people and moves further away as we get older. Our accommodation becomes more and more limited as we get older.

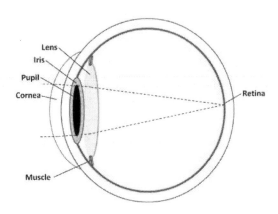

Long Sightedness (Hypermetropia)

A long-sighted eye can only see distant objects clear Images of nearby objects are formed behind the retina. The near point of the hypermetropia eye is farther away than for a normal eye. This defect is corrected using a converging meniscus 1m which converges the rays from a near object so that they appear to come from a virtual image at the near point. The eye can focus on this image because it is further away than the real object.

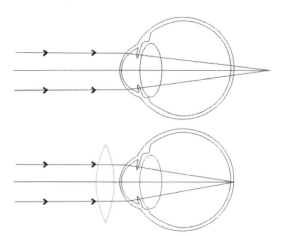

Short Sightedness (Myopia)

A myopic or short-sighted eye can only see nearby object clearly. Images of distant objects are formed in front of the retina. The eyeball may be too long or the cone lens too powerful. The far point (FP) of the myopic eye is nearer than for a normal eye. The defect is corrected using a diverging lens which diverges the rays from a distant object so that they appear to come from a virtual image at the far point. The eye can focus on this virtual image.

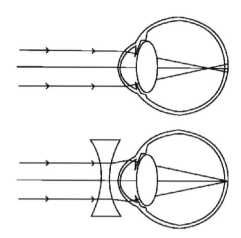

CHAPTER 7

Sound

Sound is a longitudinal wave which can travel through gases (air), liquids (under water) or solids (the Earth). Sound cannot travel through a vacuum.

When an object vibrates (moves backwards and forwards) in air, it produces sound waves. In some places the air particles are closer together - a compression. In other places the particles are further apart - a rarefaction.

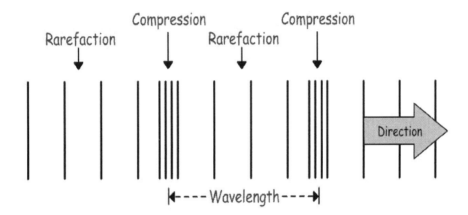

The sound wave will have the same frequency as the frequency of the vibrating object which made it.

The speed of a sound wave depends on the density of the medium through which it is travelling. The denser the medium, the faster the sound wave will travel. Sound travels the fastest through solids (as the particles are closer together) and the slowest through gases (as the particles are the furthest apart).

Speed of sound depends on elasticity of materials (its ability of its molecules to return to its original position after being displaced). When sound wave passes through air, the air is compressed and must then expand again to be ready for the next compression. The velocity of sound increases with the increase in elasticity.

The speed sound in air depend on temperature

$$v \propto \sqrt{T}$$

Sound Speed = Frequency × Wavelength

$$v = f \times \lambda$$

The equation can be rearranged to give

$$f = v \div \lambda \quad \text{or} \quad \lambda = v \div f$$

Echo

Sound which has been reflected is called an echo. As with other waves, sound reflection best occurs from flat, hard surfaces.

The natural echo of a room is called reverberation. This is a measure of how much the sound is reflected around the room.

Materials which are soft and uneven (like curtains, carpets and cushions) absorb sound much more than they reflect it, and decrease reverberation. Reflected ultrasound is used for range and direction finding, scanning and cleaning.

Loudness, Pitch and Quality

The loudness of sound depends on the amplitude of the wave. The bigger the amplitude, the louder is the sound.

The pitch of sound (how high the note is) depends on the frequency of the wave. The higher the frequency, the higher is the pitch.

The quality of a note, or how pure a note is, depends upon the note's waveform. The note from a tuning fork or a signal generator would produce a pure waveform.

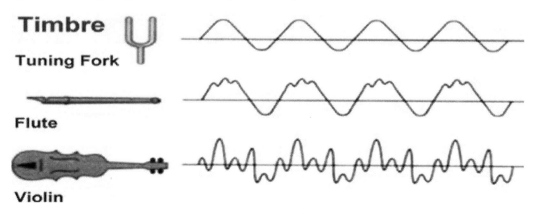

Musical instruments would produce a waveform that is a mixture of different frequencies - a more impure waveform.

The loudness of sounds - decibel levels

The chart shows some of the approximate sound levels. You can see that really loud sound scan actually be very dangerous. Loud music played through an earpiece may be a particular problem. The distance from the sound source to your ears is very important. The further away you are the better.

$$dB = 10 \log_{10}\left(\frac{Intensity}{Intensity\ at\ threshold}\right)$$

Intensity of sound of threshold of Hearing = 1×10^{-12} W/m^2

Intensity = power/area

Decibel level	Typical sound source
140	Jet taking off. Permanent hearing damage possible.
130	Jet engine at 30m, Air raid siren. Very loud rock group! Pain.
120	Pneumatic road drill, Jet engine at 150m Damage to hair cells in the inner ear.
100	Heavy road traffic.
80	Alarm clock
60	Normal conversation at 1m.
50	Quiet street.

40	Quiet radio in a house.
30	Rustle of paper. Tick of watch when held to your ear.
20	Whisper. Quiet country lane.
10	Rustle of leaves in a light breeze.
0	Threshold of hearing.

Human Hearing

Sound frequencies between 20 and 20,000 Hz can be heard by people. As people get older, the higher frequencies become more difficult to hear. Hearing can be damaged by being close to very loud sounds over a long period of time. Hearing very loud machinery or music when you are young can result in less sensitive hearing when you are older.

Unwanted sound is sometimes called noise pollution. Noise pollution can cause serious distress.

If you live near an airport or railway, the noise can be reduced by having good double glazing in the windows. If someone is working with noisy power tools, they can wear ear defenders (which look like headphones or ear muffs).

Ultrasound

Sound with a frequency higher than 20,000 Hz is called ultrasound. Ultrasound echoes are used in Scanning and Range and Direction Finding.

Ultrasound in liquids can be used to clean precious or delicate items because the compressions and rarefactions will shake dirt and unwanted material free without the risk of damage being caused by handling the item.

Ultrasound Scanning

The difference in time between emitted and reflected ultrasound waves can be used to show how far away the reflecting surface is.

When ultrasound is directed at the human body, the surfaces of different tissues inside the body partially reflect the ultrasound. A detector will receive ultrasound echoes at different times, depending on how deep inside the body the tissue surfaces are. The detector produces electrical signals which are sent to a computer and then displayed on a screen as a picture.

Ultrasound scans can safely be used to see an image of a developing baby inside the uterus of a pregnant mother. This is called "pre-natal scanning" and is useful to show if the baby is healthy. A similar technique can be used in industry to show cracks or flaws inside metal objects.

Range and Direction Finding

A boat on the sea can send a beam of ultrasound down to the sea floor where it is reflected upwards to a detector on the boat.

If both the speed of sound in the water and the time taken for the ultrasound echo to get back to the boat are known, then the depth of the sea water at that place can be calculated since

distance = speed × time.

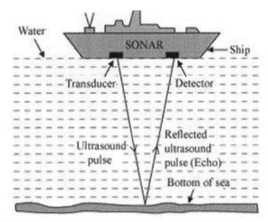

Ultrasound can be used by fishing boats to find fish, since a shoal of fish between the boat and the sea floor will return the echo more quickly.

$$Depth\ of\ sea = \frac{Speed\ of\ sound\ \times Time}{2}$$

Bats use ultrasound echoes to build up an image of their environment in darkness. They can locate insects for food in the air and know their speed and direction by analysing the reflected sound.

Ultrasound in Medicine

The most obvious use in human and veterinary medicine is the use of the ultrasound test in pregnancy.

The ultrasound equipment consists of:

- a transducer (probe), which converts electrical signals into ultrasound, and detects the reflected signals that come back.

- a signal generator that makes pulses, typically at a frequency of 1-10 megahertz.
- a computer to convert the pattern of signals back into a meaningful picture.

The transducer is coupled to the skin using a jelly. This is because ultrasound is reflected as soon as it hits a material-air boundary. Therefore, without a jelly the waves would reflect as soon as they were transmitted, and not show anything. The sonographer (operator) moves the transducer about to get patterns of signals from a wide area.

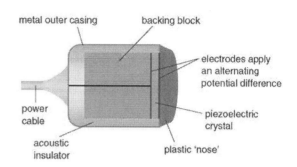

The beam of ultrasound can be focused to improve the picture. The higher the frequency, the better the resolution. Ultrasound probes can be used to break up gallstones. In dentistry, ultrasonic probes can clean plaque off your teeth.

Ultrasound in Industry

A common use for ultrasound is to check for flaws in castings. Flaws are bubbles of gas that can occur while metal is cast. As the metal solidifies, the bubbles get trapped. They can seriously weaken the casting. If they are bad enough, the casting may have to be scrapped.

The ultrasound probe sends pulses through the casting. Where the pulses meet a boundary, for example, if there are two layers of metal, they are partially reflected. If there is a flaw, most of the waves get reflected.

Seismic Waves

There are several different kinds of seismic waves and they all move in different ways. The two main types of waves are **body waves** (Primary waves and Secondary waves) and **surface waves**. Body waves can travel through the earth's inner layers, but surface waves can only move along the surface of the planet like ripples on water. Earthquakes radiate seismic energy as both body and surface waves.

Primary waves (P waves)

This is the fastest kind of seismic wave, and, consequently, the first to 'arrive' at a seismic station. The P wave can move through solid rock and fluids, like water or the liquid layers of the earth. It is a longitudinal wave which is a compression wave. It pushes and pulls the rock it moves through just like sound waves push and pull the air.

Push and pull

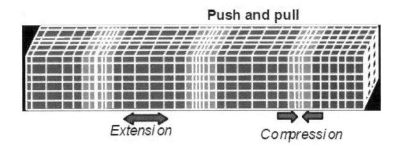

Extension   Compression

Secondary waves (S waves)

An S wave is slower than a P wave and can only move through solid rock, not through any liquid medium. It is this property of S waves that led seismologists to conclude that the Earth's outer core is a liquid. S waves move rock particles up and down, or side-to-side perpendicular to the direction that the wave is traveling in (the direction of wave propagation).

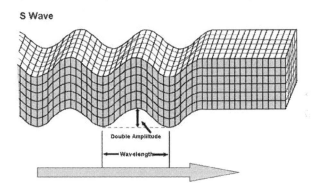

Surface waves

Travelling only through the crust, surface waves are of a lower frequency than body waves and are easily distinguished on a seismogram as a result. Though they arrive after body waves, it is surface waves that are almost entirely responsible for the damage and destruction associated with earthquakes. This damage and the strength of the surface waves are reduced in deeper earthquakes.

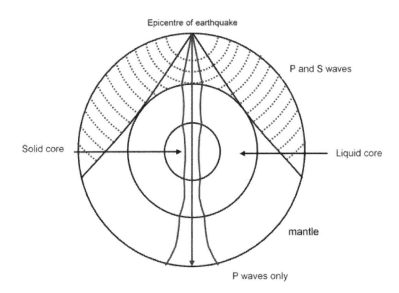

Examples

39. A thunder clap is heard 4 s after the lightning flash is seen. How far away is the storm centre?

We could only proximate the distance, as the speed of light is not infinity.

Distance = speed × time = 340 × 4 = 1360 m

40. A man standing 504 m from a cliff claps his hands and hears the echo 3 s later. What value doe s this observation gives for the velocity of sound in air?

Echo is sound reflection, therefore, the total distance travelled is 504 + 504 = 1008 m

$$speed = \frac{distance}{time} = \frac{1008}{3} = 336 \; m/s$$

41. ship using an echo-sounding device receives an echo from a wreck 0.8s after the sound is transmitted. If the velocity of sound in sea-water is 1500 m s-1, what is the depth of the wreck?

depth = speed × time/2 = 1500 × 0.8/2 = 600 m

42. The timekeeper for a 100 m race stands at the finishing tape and starts his watch when he hears the starting pistol. If his recorded time is 14 s, what is the correct time for the winner?

$$\textbf{\textit{The time taken for sound to travel to timekeeper}} = \frac{distance}{speed} = \frac{100}{340}$$

$$= 0.29 \; s$$

The correct time = 14 + 0.29 = 14.29 d

43. The diagram shows a cross-section through the Earth.

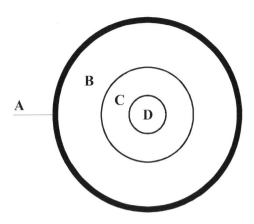

(a)   Name the parts labelled **A**, **B**, **C** and **D**.

    A .... crust.....................

    B .... mantle.................

    C .... outer core.........

    D ....inner core.........

(b)   The diagram below shows the way a building vibrates when an earth tremor is first felt.
The vibrations are caused by P and S waves (seismic waves) which travel through the mantle.

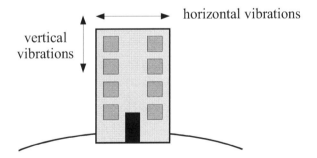

The building vibrates vertically at first. A very short time later it begins to vibrate horizontally as well.
Explain why.

   P waves travel faster than S waves

   P waves are longitudinal which cause vertical vibrations

   S waves are transverse which cause horizontal vibrations

(c) Information about the Earth's structure has been obtained by studying the shock (seismic) waves produced by earthquakes.
The diagrams show the paths of seismic waves through the mantle and the core.

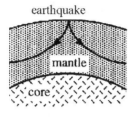
diagram **X**

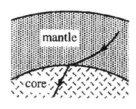
diagram **Y**

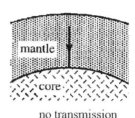
diagram **Z**

(i) Describe and explain what happens to both waves travelling through the mantle in diagram **X**.

Waves refract due to a gradual increase in density; the velocity of the wave velocity increases with the increase in density.

(ii) Describe and explain what happens to the wave travelling from the mantle to the core in diagram **Y**.
State which type of wave is shown.

P waves refract due to change in density, which result in a change in direction.

(iii) Explain why the wave shown in diagram **Z** does not travel through the core.
State which type of wave is shown.

S waves are transverse waves which means they cannot travel in liquid.

CHAPTER 8

Doppler Effect

The Doppler Effect is the apparent change of frequency and wavelength when a source of waves and an observer move relative to each other.

One of the most important applications of the Doppler Effect is in the study of the expansion of the Universe. Galaxies have their light shifted towards the red due to their speed of recession and when we receive the light at the Earth we describe it as Red Shifted.

The Doppler theory in Wave Motion

Consider a source S moving from left to right. Initially, it is at position 1 and sometime later at positions 2 and 3. If it is emitting a wave, then the three circles represent the positrons of the waves emitted at points 1, 2 and 3 sometime after the source past position 3. You can see that the wavelengths on the right are closer together than those on the left; if the source is approaching an observer, the wavelength will be reduced while if it is moving away they will be increased.

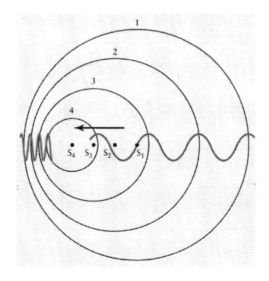

Doppler Ultrasound

Doppler ultrasound is based on the shift of frequency in an ultrasound wave caused by a moving reflector, such as blood cells in the vasculature (Fig. below). This is the same effect that causes a siren on a police car to sound high pitched as the car approaches the listener (the wavelength is compressed) and a shift to a lower pitch sound as it passes by and continues on (the wavelength is expanded). The moving reflectors in the body are the blood cells. By comparing the incident ultrasound frequency with the reflected ultrasound frequency from the blood cells, it is possible to detect the velocity of the blood.

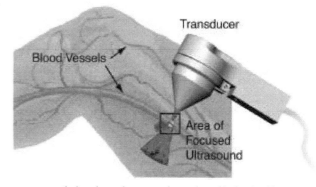

Red-Shift

The big bang theory developed as an attempt to explain the observation that light in line spectra from other galaxies is red-shifted. This means that light from other galaxies appears to be at a longer wavelength than it is on Earth.

It is called a red-shift because the colour red is at the longer wavelength end of the visible light spectrum. If light appeared to be at a shorter wavelength, it would be called a blue-shift. It is accepted by scientists as a fact that light from other galaxies has a red-shift. The further away the galaxy, the greater the red-shift. The fact that this light is at a longer wavelength than expected requires an explanation.

The Big Bang

The Big Bang is the dominant theory of the origin of the universe. This theory states that the universe began from an initial point or singularity which has expanded over 15 billion years to form the universe as we now know it. All the energy and matter which exists today came from this original explosion.

Immediately following the Big Bang, the universe was very hot. Eventually, the universe cooled sufficiently that protons and electrons could combine to form neutral hydrogen. This occurred roughly 400,000 years after the Big Bang when the universe was about one eleven hundredth its present size. Cosmic microwave background photons interact very weakly with neutral hydrogen, allowing them to travel in a straight line.

The cosmic background radiation (CBR) is the afterglow of the big bang. The wavelength of the afterglow increased as the universe expanded. This caused the radiation originally produced in the big bang to redshift to longer wavelengths in the microwave range of electromagnetic radiation. It fills the universe, falling on Earth from every direction with nearly uniform intensity.

Expanding Universe

A red-shift means that other galaxies are moving away from us. When light is emitted from an object, it will have a particular wavelength. The wavelength will change if the object is moving towards you or away from you.

Imagine that an object which is moving towards you is emitting a wavelength of 1.0 metres. During the time it has taken to emit one complete wave, the object might have moved 0.1 metres towards you. The wavelength has been shortened because the whole wave now only takes 0.9 metres. The faster the object is moving towards you, the more the wavelength is decreased. A decrease in the wavelength of light is called a blue shift.

Imagine that the same object is now moving away from you at the same speed. During the time it has taken to emit one complete wave, the object would have moved 0.1 metres away from you. The wavelength has been increased because the whole wave now takes up 1.1 metres. An increase in the wavelength of light is called a red- shift.

In summary, light from an object:

- Moving fast towards you - wavelength decreases - blue-shift.
- Which is stationary - wavelength stays the same - no shift.
- Moving fast away from you - wavelength increases - red-shift.

Since the light from other galaxies is red-shifted, these other galaxies must be moving away from us very quickly. The further away the galaxy is, the greater the red-shift and the greater the speed at which it is moving away from us.

REVISION QUESTIONS

44. (a) Thermal energy (heat) can be transferred by **conduction, convection, radiation** and **evaporation.**

    Complete the following sentence about thermal energy (heat) transfer.

    Transfer of thermal energy by a metal, without the metal itself moving, is

    called ....

    (b) Explain what is meant by convection.

    (c) The diagram shows a vacuum (Thermos) flask. It is used to keep drinks hot for a long time.

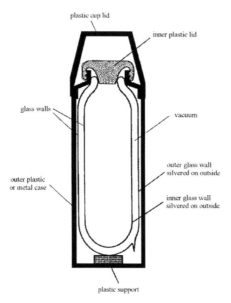

    Use some of the labelled parts of the diagram to answer the following questions.

    (i) Give **two** ways in which heat loss by conduction is kept low.

        1

        2

    (ii) Give **two** ways in which heat loss by radiation is kept low.

1

2

45.   (a)   The diagram shows hot water being poured into a mug.

(i)   Complete the sentence by choosing the correct words from the box. Each word   may be used once or not at all.

air	mug	table	water

Heat energy is being transferred from the .... to

the ....

(ii)   When will this transfer of heat energy stop?

(b)   In the box are the names of four types of fuel used to heat homes.

coal	gas	oil	wood

Which **one** of these types of fuel is renewable?

(c)   The diagram shows where heat energy is lost from a house.

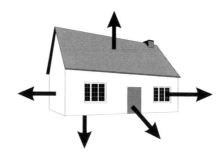

(i) Complete the sentences by choosing the correct words from the box. Each word   may be used once or not at all.

| conduction | conductor | convection | electric | evaporation | insulator |

The   amount   of   heat   energy   lost   through   the   windows   by

.... can be reduced by using thick curtains. The

curtains trap a layer of air and air is a good

....

The curtains will also stop .... currents pulling

cold air into the room through small gaps in the window.

(iii) Write down **one** other way of reducing heat loss from a house.

46. (a) The drawing shows the energy transferred each second by a television set.

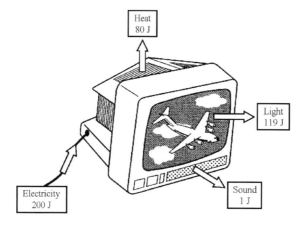

(i)   What form of energy is transferred as waste energy by the television set?

(ii)   What effect will the waste energy have on the air around the television set?

(iii) Use the following equation to calculate the efficiency of the television set.

$$\text{efficiency} = \frac{\text{useful energy transferred by device}}{\text{total energy supplied to device}}$$

Efficiency = ...

(b)   The diagrams show the energy transferred each second for three different types of lamp. For each lamp the electrical energy input each second is 100 joules.

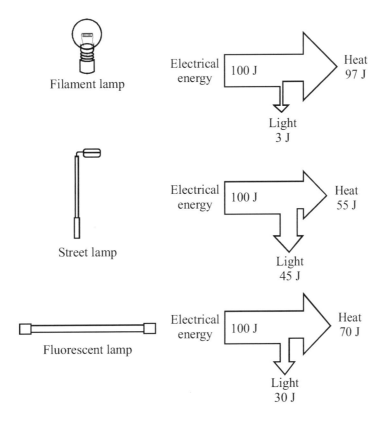

Which type of lamp is the most efficient?

Give a reason for your choice.

47.   The drawing shows water being heated in a metal saucepan.

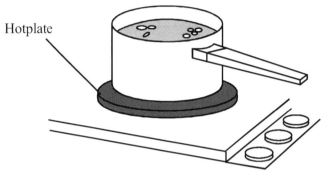

Hotplate

(a)   Explain, in terms of the particles in the metal, how heat energy is transferred through the base of the saucepan.

(b)   Energy is transferred through the water by convection currents. Explain what happens to cause a convection current in the water. The answer has been started for you.

As heat energy is transferred through the saucepan, the water particles at the bottom

(c)   Some energy is transferred from the hotplate to the air by *thermal radiation*. What is meant by *thermal radiation*?

(b)   move faster or take up more space

48. How much heat energy is needed to raise the temperature of a 400 g piece of lead by 200 °C?

49. A 800 g potato cools from 100 °C to 50 °C. If the specific heat capacity of potato is 2000 J/kg°C how much heat does the potato loose?

50. A 900 g copper saucepan contains 2 kg of water. If the water and the saucepan are heated from 20 °C to 100 °C, calculate:

(a) how much heat energy the water gains

(b) how much heat energy the saucepan gains

(c) the total energy needed to heat the water and saucepan.

51. A small piece of aluminium of mass 200 g is used on a circuit that has a normal temperature of 20 °C. If the piece of aluminium must not get hotter than 150 °C how much heat energy can it absorb? Specific heat capacity = 902 J/kg °C

52. Why do you think that houses built of stone take a long time to warm up but once they are warm they stay warm for a long time?

53. A pie is cooked in an oven at 200 °C. The aluminium film that covered the pie can be touched soon after it is removed while the pie is still dangerously hot. Explain this.

54. How long will it take a 100 W heater to melt 3kg of ice at 0^0C?

[Specific latent heat of fusion of ice = 335 000 J/kg.]

*55. (a) A copper saucepan of mass 850g is filled with 2kg of water at 18°C. A 800W heater is then placed in the water and switched on for 10 minutes. Specific heat capacity of water is 4200 and for copper is 385 J/kg°C

56. How much heat is needed to heat 150g of water at 15°C to steam at 100°C? Specific latent heat of vaporisation of water = 2 300 000 J/kg and specific heat capacity of water is 4200.

*57. A hot copper rivet of mass 200g is dropped into 500g of water initially at 16°C. If the water temperature rises to 35°C what was the initial temperature of the rivet?

58. How does the high value of the specific heat capacity of water help to reduce the variation in temperature of land masses adjacent to oceans?

59.Why is a scald by steam at 100°C much more painful than one by water at 100°C?

60. A piece of lead of mass 500 g and at air temperature falls from a height of 25 m. What is:

(a) its initial potential energy;

(b) its kinetic energy on reaching the ground?

61. A waterfall is 100 m high and the difference in temperature between the water at the top and that at the bottom is 0.24 °C. Obtain a value for the specific heat capacity of water, explaining the steps in your calculations. Mention any assumptions you make.

*62. Some hot water was added to three times its mass of water at 10 °C and the resulting temperature was 20 °C What was the temperature of the hot water?

63.The diagram below shows a vacuum flask.

   (a)   Give **two** features of the flask which reduce heat loss by conduction.

   (b)   Give **one** feature of the flask which reduces heat loss by radiation.
         Silvering of inside wall

64. Describe briefly an experiment to illustrate each of the following:

   a) water is a bad conductor of heat,

   b) copper is a better conductor of heat than iron,

   c) convection currents in gases,

   d) a rough surface is a better emitter of radiation than a polished surface.

65. A ray of light travelling from air to glass makes an angle of incidence of 30°. Find the angle of refraction, if the refractive index for glass is 1.5.

66. A ray of light travelling from toluene to air has an angle of incidence of $27°$ and an angle of refraction of $42°$. What value does this give for the refractive index of toluene?

67. A gas jar contains paraffin to a depth of 21.6 cm. Its apparent depth is found to be 15.0 cm. What is the refractive index of paraffin?

68. A block of glass 60 mm thick is placed on top of an ink spot. How far is the spot apparently displaced?

69. If light travels at 3.00×10^8 ms^{-1} in a vacuum what is its speed in glass of refractive index 1.5?

*70. Light of wavelength 6.0×10^{-7}m in a vacuum enters the glass. what is its wavelength in the glass? Refractive index of glass = 1.5

*71. A fish is at a depth of 2.0 m in a canal with a vertical bank and is 1.5m from the bank. The water is level with the banks. How close to the bank can an angler 1.8 m tall stand before he is just seen by the fish?

The refractive index of water = 1.5

Refractive index of air = 1

72. Find the critical angle for (a) water of refractive index 4/3, (b) diamond of refractive index 2.42.

73. A ray of light is incident normally on a glass prism of refracting angle $30°$. What is the deviation of the ray?

74. What happens to the frequency of light as it passes from air into a material with a higher refractive index?

75. A transparent material has an absolute refractive index of 1.45. What is the speed of light in the material?

76. Light travelling in the core of a glass fibre at 2×10^8 ms^{-1} meets the interface with the cladding of the fibre in which the speed of light is 2.4×10^8 ms^{-1}. What is the critical angle for the core-cladding interface?

77. Calculate the critical angle for:

(a) Plastic of refractive index 1.45 in air

(b) A plastic water interface - refractive index of water 1.33

78. An object 4 cm high is at right angles to the principal axis of a diverging lens of focal length 20 cm and at 30 cm from it. Determine the position of the image and its size.

79. An illuminated object 1.05 cm long is placed on and at right angles to the axis of a converging lens and an image 0.35 cm long is formed on a screen suitably placed at a distance of 80 cm from the object. Find the position of the lens and its focal length

80. A convex lens is used to project an image of a light source on to a screen. The screen is 30 cm from the light source, and the image is twice the size of the object. What focal length lens is required, and how far from the source must it be placed?

81. An object 37.5 cm from a lens produces a real image 75.0 cm from the lens. What type of lens is it, and what is its focal length?

As the image is real image, the lens is convex lens.

82. The diagram represents the structure of the Earth.

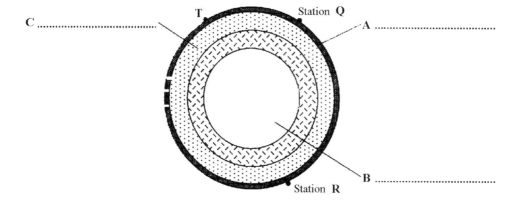

(a) On the diagram, name the parts **A** to **C**.

(b) An earthquake occurs at the point **T** on the Earth's surface.
Two types of shock wave are produced by the earthquake, P waves and S waves.

Describe **two** similarities and **two** differences between P waves and S waves as they travel through the Earth.

Similarities:

Differences:

(c)   State whether P waves or S waves or both will reach:

(i)   Station Q;

(ii)   Station R.

83.   (a)   All radio waves travel at 300 000 000 m/s in air.

(i)   Give the equation that links the frequency, speed and wavelength of a wave.

(ii)   Calculate the wavelength, in metres, of a radio wave which is broadcast at a frequency of 909 kHz. Show clearly how you work out your answer.

(b)   The diagram shows what happens to the radio waves of part (a) as they approach and pass a hill.

(i)   What is the name given to the process which changes the shape of the waves?

(ii)   Explain why the person living in the house is unlikely to be able to receive television signals broadcast at a frequency of 550 000 kHz, even though they have the correct aerial.

(b)   Earthquakes produce longitudinal **P** and transverse **S** waves which travel through the Earth. These waves are recorded at earthquake stations around the world.

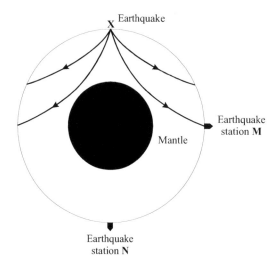

(i)   Why do **P** and **S** waves follow curved paths?

(ii)   The diagram shows the seismic chart recorded at earthquake station **M** following an earthquake at **X**.

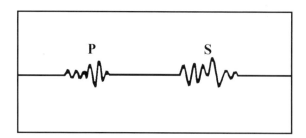

How would the seismic chart recorded at earthquake station **N** be different to that recorded at station **M**?

Explain your answer.

84.   (a)   A signal generator connected to a loudspeaker produces a sound wave. With the frequency of the signal generator set to 2000 Hz the sound wave has a wavelength of 0.17 m in air.

Calculate the speed of sound in air.

(b)   The speed of sound in water is 1400 m/s.

A sound wave has a frequency of 2000 Hz. Calculate its wavelength in water.

(c) Echo sounders are used at sea to locate underwater objects, such as submarines.

The diagram below shows how an echo sounder works.

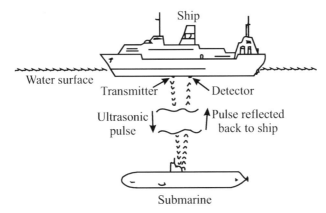

(i)   What are ultrasonic waves?

(ii) The pulse travels from the transmitter to the submarine and back to the detector. The time taken is 0.1 s.

Calculate the distance between the submarine and the ship.

(iii) State **one** other use for ultrasonic waves.

85. The diagram shows the electromagnetic spectrum.

Gamma rays	X-rays	Ultra violet	Visible light	Infra red	Microwaves	Radio

(a) Name the type of electromagnetic radiation which is used:

(i)   to prevent fresh food going bad quickly. ....

(ii) to heat passengers' meals in an aeroplane. ....

(b) (i)   State **one** use of X-rays.

(ii) State **one** use of ultra violet radiation.

(c)   Longer wavelength radio waves are used for communications over very long distances without using satellites. Explain why this is possible.

86.   (a)   In the box are the names of five waves.

infra red   microwaves   ultrasonic   ultraviolet   X-rays

Which wave is used to:

(i)   send information to a satellite,

(ii)   (ii) toast bread

(iii)   clean a valuable ring?

(b)   The diagram shows four oscilloscope wave traces. The controls of the oscilloscope were the same for each wave trace.

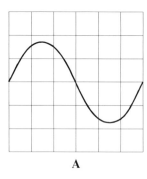

A

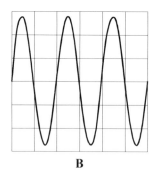

B

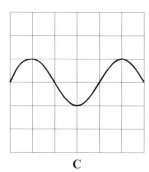

C

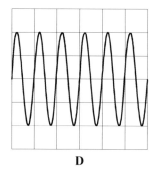

D

Which **one** of the waves traces, **A**, **B**, **C** or **D**, has:

(i)   the largest amplitude,

(ii)   the lowest frequency?

(c)   The diagram shows a longitudinal wave in a stretched spring.

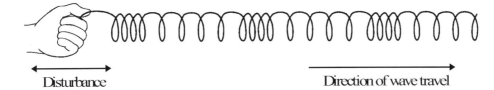

Disturbance   Direction of wave travel

Complete the sentence. You should put only **one** word in each space.

A longitudinal wave is one in which the …vibrations... causing the wave is in

the same......direction............. as that in which the wave moves.

(d)   Which **one** of the following types of wave is longitudinal? Draw a ring around your answer.

light wave   **sound wave**   **water wave**

87.   Explain how observations at the red end of the spectrum of light from galaxies have led to one theory about the origin of the Universe.

88.   (a)   The Big Bang theory attempts to explain the origin of the Universe.

(i)   What is the Universe?

(i)   What are the main ideas of the Big Bang theory?

(iii)   What is thought to be happening to the size of the Universe?

(b)   Most of the Sun is hydrogen. Inside the core of the sun, hydrogen is being converted to helium. What name is given to this process and why is the process so important?

Describe what will happen to the Sun as the core runs out of hydrogen.

REVISION QUESTIONS ANSWERS

44. (a) Thermal energy (heat) can be transferred by **conduction, convection, radiation** and **evaporation.**

Complete the following sentence about thermal energy (heat) transfer.

Transfer of thermal energy by a metal, without the metal itself moving, is called
....*conduction*.............. .

 (b) Explain what is meant by convection.

Convection is the transfer of heat by the movement of molecules. This only happens liquid and gas. The hot liquid or gas expands and increases in volume. The density of the hot liquid or gas decreases and it starts to rise upwards. The colder liquid or gas replaces it. This cycle is repeated.

(c) The diagram shows a vacuum (Thermos) flask. It is used to keep drinks hot for a long time.

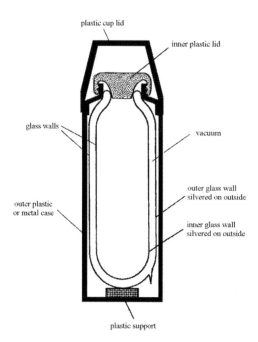

Use some of the labelled parts of the diagram to answer the following questions.

(i) Give **two** ways in which heat loss by conduction is kept low.

1   Vacuum between inside glass and outside glass

2   Plastic insulation between the outer glass plastic or metal case.

(ii) Give **two** ways in which heat loss by radiation is kept low.

   1.   Outer glass is silvered

   2.   Inner glass is silvered

45. (a) The diagram shows hot water being poured into a mug.

(i)   Complete the sentence by choosing the correct words from the box. Each word   may be used once or not at all.

air	mug	table	water

Heat energy is being transferred from the ....*mug*.. to

the ....*air and table*... .

(ii) When will this transfer of heat energy stop?

   when temperatures are the same

 (b) In the box are the names of four types of fuel used to heat homes.

coal	gas	oil	wood

Which **one** of these types of fuel is renewable?

......................*Wood*...

(c) The diagram shows where heat energy is lost from a house.

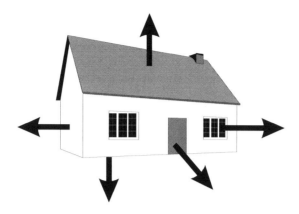

(i) Complete the sentences by choosing the correct words from the box. Each word may be used once or not at all.

conduction	conductor	convection	electric	evaporation	insulator

The amount of heat energy lost through the windows by ....Conduction................ can be reduced by using thick curtains.

The curtains trap a layer of air and air is a good ...insulator......... .

The curtains will also stop ....convection....... currents pulling

cold air into the room through small gaps in the window.

(ii) Write down **one** other way of reducing heat loss from a house.

double glazing, loft insulation, carpets

cavity wall insulation, draft excluders

46. (a) The drawing shows the energy transferred each second by a television set.

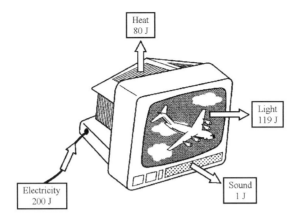

(i) What form of energy is transferred as waste energy by the television set?

..................Heat...

(ii) What effect will the waste energy have on the air around the television set?

...............Temperature Increase causes convection currents.........

(iii) Use the following equation to calculate the efficiency of the television set.

$$efficiency = \frac{useful\ energy\ transferred\ by\ device}{total\ energy\ supplied\ to\ device}$$

$$efficiency = \frac{119+1}{200} = 0.6\ or\ 60\%$$

(b) The diagrams show the energy transferred each second for three different types of lamp. For each lamp the electrical energy input each second is 100 joules.

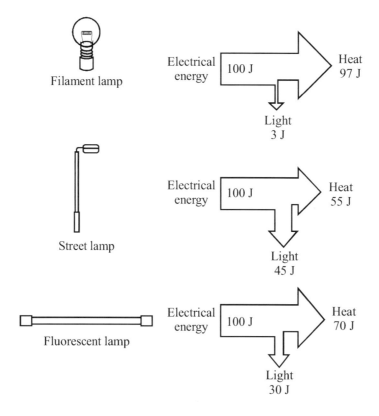

Filament lamp

Electrical energy 100 J → Heat 97 J

Light 3 J

Street lamp

Electrical energy 100 J → Heat 55 J

Light 45 J

Fluorescent lamp

Electrical energy 100 J → Heat 70 J

Light 30 J

Which type of lamp is the most efficient?

...........................Street...

Give a reason for your choice.
    Less energy wasted compare with bulbs. Higher energy output.

47.   The drawing shows water being heated in a metal saucepan.

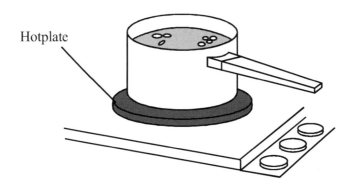

Hotplate

(a)   Explain, in terms of the particles in the metal, how heat energy is transferred through the base of the saucepan.

When the base is heated, the amount by which the particles vibrate is increased. The increase in energy is passed on to the next particle through collisions with the next particle, which in turn starts to vibrate more and collide with next one. Delocalised electrons take most of the heat from the bottom of the pan to the top surface of base.

(b)   Energy is transferred through the water by convection currents. Explain what happens to cause a convection current in the water. The answer has been started for you.

As heat energy is transferred through the saucepan, the water particles at the bottom

As particles move faster or take up more space, warmer water expands and becomes less dense. Warm water rises through colder water and the colder water falls to take its place

(c)   Some energy is transferred from the hotplate to the air by *thermal radiation*. What is meant by *thermal radiation*?

transfer of energy by infrared radiation

48. How much heat energy is needed to raise the temperature of a 400 g piece of lead by 200 °C?

$$E = m \times c \times \theta = 0.4 \times 4200 \times 200 = 336000\,J$$

49. A 800 g potato cools from 100 °C to 50 °C. If the specific heat capacity of potato is 2000 J/kg°C how much heat does the potato loose?

$$E = m \times c \times \theta = 0.8 \times 2000 \times 50 = 80000\,J$$

50. A 900 g copper saucepan contains 2 kg of water. If the water and the saucepan are heated from 20 °C to 100 °C, calculate:

(a) how much heat energy the water gains

(b) how much heat energy the saucepan gains

(c) the total energy needed to heat the water and saucepan.

a) $E = m \times c \times \theta = 2 \times 4200 \times 80 = 672000\,J$

b) $E = m \times c \times \theta = 0.9 \times 385 \times 80 = 27720\,J$

c) $E = 672000 + 27720 = 699720\,J$

51. A small piece of aluminium of mass 200 g is used on a circuit that has a normal temperature of 20 °C. If the piece of aluminium must not get hotter than 150 °C how much heat energy can it absorb? Specific heat capacity = 902 J/kg °C

$$E = m \times c \times \theta = 0.2 \times 902 \times 130 = 23452\,J$$

52. Why do you think that houses built of stone take a long time to warm up but once they are warm they stay warm for a long time?

Stone has high specific heat capacity

53. A pie is cooked in an oven at 200 °C. The aluminium film that covered the pie can be touched soon after it is removed while the pie is still dangerously hot. Explain this.

Aluminium has small heat capacity compared to the pie. The pie is mainly water and has high specific heat capacity. Water has specific heat capacity which is more than four times the specific heat capacity of aluminium. Therefore, the pie has four times more energy compare to foil.

54. How long will it take a 100 W heater to melt 3kg of ice at 0^0C?

[Specific latent heat of fusion of ice = 335 000 J/kg.]

Energy needed to melt the ice = 3 × 335000 = 1005000 J

Power = Energy / time

time = Energy/power = 1005000 /100 = 10050 s = 167.5 minutes

The real time, measured experimentally, is less the calculated time. Why is that?

*55. (a) A copper saucepan of mass 850g is filled with 2kg of water at 18°C. A 800W heater is then placed in the water and switched on for 10 minutes. Specific heat capacity of water is 4200 and for copper is 385 J/kg°C

What is the temperature of the water after this time?

The temperature saucepan and water inside it are always the same.

Energy generated by the heater = Energy absorbed by water and saucepan

Energy absorbed by water + Energy absorbed by copper = 2 × 4200 × (θ-18) + 0.85 × 385 × (θ-18)

Energy generated by the heater = 800 × 10 × 60 = 480000 J

480000 = (8400+ 327.25) (θ-18)

(θ-18) = 55

θ = 73 °C

56. How much heat is needed to heat 150g of water at 15°C to steam at 100°C? Specific latent heat of vaporisation of water = 2 300 000 J/kg and specific heat capacity of water is 4200.

Energy required to heat the water from 15 to 100 °C = $m \times c \times \theta$ = 0.15 × 4200 × 85 = 53550 J

Energy required to change water at 100 °C to steam at 100 °C = $m \times l_v$ =0.15×2300000 = 345000 J

Total energy = 345000 + 53550 =398550 J

*57. A hot copper rivet of mass 200g is dropped into 500g of water initially at 16°C. If the water temperature rises to 35°C what was the initial temperature of the rivet?

Assuming there was no heat loss, then

The energy released by rivet = energy absorbed by water

0.2 × 385 × (θ-35) = 0.5 × 4200 ×(35-16)

(θ-35) = 39900 / 77 = 518.18

$\theta = 518.18 + 35 = 553.18\ °C$

58. How does the high value of the specific heat capacity of water help to reduce the variation in temperature of land masses adjacent to oceans?

During the day, the sun heats the land and ocean. As it takes a large amount of energy to heat the oceans by a few degrees, the change in temperature on land and ocean is small. During the night, the land and ocean will cool down. During the night, the ocean will produce a large amount of energy for a small change in temperature which will keep the temperature change small during day or night.

59. Why is a scald by steam at 100°C much more painful than one by water at 100°C?

Each 1 kg of steam at 100 °C has 2300000 J more energy than water at 100 °C.

60. A piece of lead of mass 500 g and at air temperature falls from a height of 25 m. What is:

(a) its initial potential energy;

(b) its kinetic energy on reaching the ground?

If all the energy becomes internal energy in the lead when it strikes the ground, calculate the rise in temperature of the lead if its specific heat capacity is 130 J/kg °C.

    a. PE = mgh = 0.5 × 10 × 25 = 125 J

    b. KE on the lowest point = PE on the highest point = 125 J

        E = m×c×θ

$$\theta = \frac{E}{mc} = \frac{125}{0.5 \times 130} = 1.92\ °C$$

61. A waterfall is 100 m high and the difference in temperature between the water at the top and that at the bottom is 0.24 °C. Obtain a value for the specific heat capacity of water, explaining the steps in your calculations. Mention any assumptions you make.

Firstly, we need to find the energy difference

$PE = mgh = m \times 10 \times 100 = 1000\ m$

The above PE has converted into KE and then KE converted into internal energy

$E = EP = 1000\ m = m \times c \times \theta$

$1000 = c \times 0.24,\ c = 4166.67\ J/kg\ ^{\circ}C$

*62. Some hot water was added to three times its mass of water at 10 °C and the resulting temperature was 20 °C What was the temperature of the hot water?

Volume of cold hot water = v

Volume of cold water = 3v

Energy loss from hot water = Energy gained by cold water

Using $E = m \times c \times \theta$

And $m = \rho \times V$

$E = \rho \times V \times c \times \theta$

For cold water

$E = \rho \times 3 \times v \times c \times (20-10)$

For hot water

$E = \rho \times v \times c \times (\theta-20)$

$\rho \times 3 \times v \times c \times (20-10) = \rho \times v \times c \times (\theta-20)$

$(\theta-20) = 30$

$\theta = 50\ ^{\circ}C$

63.   The diagram below shows a vacuum flask.

(a) Give **two** features of the flask which reduce heat loss by conduction.

Plastic outer cover and glass wall

(b)   Give **one** feature of the flask which reduces heat loss by radiation.

Silvering of inside wall

64. Describe briefly an experiment to illustrate each of the following:

(a) water is a bad conductor of heat,

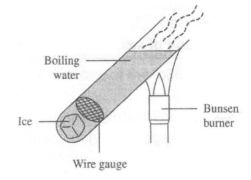

- Wedge a piece of ice at the bottom of a test tube so that it cannot float.
- Almost fill the tube with cold water and then heat it near its upper end, as shown in the diagram.
- Use a Bunsen burner to heat the top part of the test tube, just below the water level.
- The water at the top of the tube boils, while the ice at the bottom, remains unmelted.
- Eventually, the slow conduction of heat through the water and the walls of the glass test tube melts the ice

(b) copper is a better conductor of heat than iron,

- Attach small drawing pins to copper and ion rods using small amount of Vaseline.
- Use a Bunsen burner to heat the rods.
- The drawing pin attached to copper rod will drop first; this indicates that heat energy has conducted quicker through copper rod.

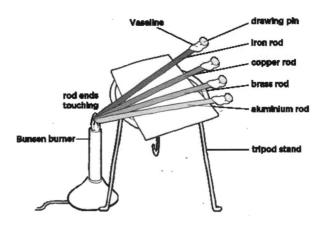

(c) convection currents in gases,

Use the arrangement below. Light the candle. Put a smouldering rag above the chimney. You will see that the smoke produced by the rag will be pulled into the box and emerges from the other chimney.

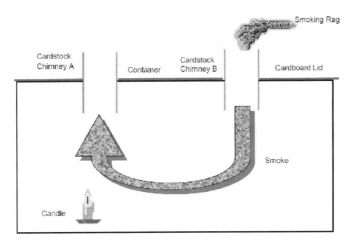

(d) a rough surface is a better emitter of radiation than a polished surface.

Use two cans, one painted matt black and the other a shiny polished surface.

- Put the same amount of water at the same temperature in each can.
- Cover with a lid and put a thermometer inside each of them to measure the temperature.
- Put both cans near a heat radiation source, like a filament bulb.
- Leave them for 10 minutes and measure the temperature. You will notice that the temperature of the black can is hotter than polished one.

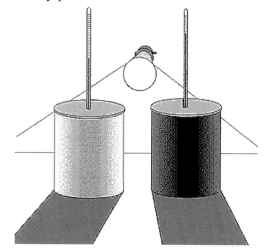

65. A stone floor feels very cold to bare feet in the winter. But a carpet, in the same room, feels comfortably warm. Why is this?

A stone floor is a good conductor of heat energy. When you walk on stone floor, heat energy from your feet will transfer to the stone floor. That is why the stone floor feels cold.

Carpet material is a good insulator; the surface pile of carpet with its millions of tiny fibres traps air and further increases its thermal insulation.

66. A ray of light travelling from air to glass makes an angle of incidence of 30°. Find the angle of refraction, if the refractive index for glass is 1.5.

$$n = \frac{sin\ i}{sin\ r}$$

$$sin\ r = \frac{sin\ i}{n}$$

$$sin\ r = \frac{sin\ 30}{1.5}$$

r = 19.5°

67. A ray of light travelling from toluene to air has an angle of incidence of 27° and an angle of refraction of 42°. What value does this give for the refractive index of toluene?

Medium 1 is toluene

Medium 2 is air

$$1n2 = \frac{n_2}{n_1} = \frac{\sin i}{\sin r}$$

$$\frac{1}{n_1} = \frac{\sin 27}{\sin 42}$$

$$n = \frac{\sin 42}{\sin 27} = 1.47$$

68. A gas jar contains paraffin to a depth of 21.6 cm. Its apparent depth is found to be 15.0 cm. What is the refractive index of paraffin?

$$Refractive\ index = \frac{real\ depth}{apparent\ depath}$$

$$Refractive\ index = \frac{21.6}{15} = 1.44$$

69. A block of glass 60 mm thick is placed on top of an ink spot. How far is the spot apparently displaced?

$$Refractive\ index = \frac{real\ depth}{apparent\ depath}$$

$$1.5 = \frac{60}{apparent\ thickness}$$

Apparent thickness = 40 mm

*70. (a) If light travels at 3.00 x 10^8 ms^{-1} in a vacuum what is its speed in glass of refractive index 1.5?

$$n = \frac{c_1}{c_2}$$

$$1.5 = \frac{3 \times 10^8}{c_2}$$

$c_2 = 2 \times 10^8$ m/s

(b) Light of wavelength 6.0 x 10^{-7}m in a vacuum enters the glass. what is its wavelength in the glass? Refractive index of glass = 1.5

$$c = \lambda f$$

$$n = \frac{c_1}{c_2} = \frac{f \lambda_1}{f \lambda_2} = \frac{\lambda_1}{\lambda_2}$$

$$1.5 = \frac{6 \times 10^{-7}}{\lambda_2}$$

$\lambda_2 = 4 \times 10^{-7}$ m

*71. A fish is at a depth of 2.0 m in a canal with a vertical bank and is 1.5m from the bank. The water is level with the banks. How close to the bank can an angler 1.8 m tall stand before he is just seen by the fish?

The refractive index of water = 1.5

Refractive index of air = 1

$$tan\ i = \frac{1.5}{2}$$

$$tan\ r = \frac{x}{1.8}$$

$$i = tan^{-1} \frac{1.5}{2} = 36.86°$$

using

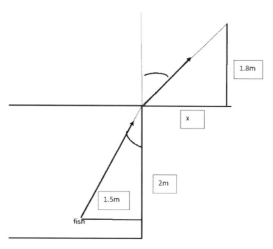

$$1n2 = \frac{n_2}{n_1} = \frac{sin\ i}{sin\ r}$$

$$\frac{1}{1.5} = \frac{\sin 36.86}{\sin r}$$

$$\sin r = 1.5 \sin 36.86 = 0.9$$

$$r = \sin^{-1} 0.9 = 64°$$

$$\tan 64 = \frac{x}{1.8}$$

$$x = 1.8 \tan 64 = 3.7 \, m$$

72. Find the critical angle for (a) water of refractive index 4/3, (b) diamond of refractive index 2.42.

$$\sin \theta_c = \frac{1}{n}$$

a)

$$\sin \theta_c = \frac{3}{4}$$

$$\theta_c = \sin^{-1} \frac{3}{4} = 48.6°$$

b)

$$\sin \theta_c = \frac{1}{2.42}$$

$$\theta_c = \sin^{-1} 0.41 = 24.4°$$

73. A ray of light is incident normally on a glass prism of refracting angle 30°. What is the deviation of the ray?

$$n = \frac{\sin i}{\sin r}$$

$$1.5 = \frac{\sin 30}{\sin r}$$

r = 19.4⁰

Deviation = 30 – 19.4 = 10.6⁰

74. What happens to the frequency of light as it passes from air into a material with a higher refractive index?

No change in frequency of light. No change in colour of light as it passes from low density to high density medium.

75. A transparent material has an absolute refractive index of 1.45. What is the speed of light in the material?

$$n = \frac{c_1}{c_2} = \frac{300000000}{c_2}$$

$$1.45 = \frac{300000000}{c_2}$$

c2 = 206,896551 m/s

76. Light travelling in the core of a glass fibre at 2×10^8 ms^{-1} meets the interface with the cladding of the fibre in which the speed of light is 2.4x10^8 ms^{-1}. What is the critical angle for the core-cladding interface?

$$\sin \theta_c = \frac{n_2}{n_1} = \frac{c_1}{c_2}$$

$$\sin \theta_c = \frac{2}{2.4} = 0.833$$

$$\theta_c = 56.44°$$

77. Calculate the critical angle for:

(a) Plastic of refractive index 1.45 in air

(b) A plastic water interface - refractive index of water 1.33

a)

$$\sin \theta_c = \frac{n_2}{n_1} = \frac{1}{1.45} = 0.69$$

$$\theta_c = 43.6°$$

b)

$$\sin \theta_c = \frac{n_2}{n_1} = \frac{1}{1.33} = 0.75$$

$$\theta_c = 48.7°$$

78. An object 4 cm high is at right angles to the principal axis of a diverging lens of focal length 20 cm and at 30 cm from it. Determine the position of the image and its size.

$$\frac{1}{f} = \frac{1}{u} + \frac{1}{v}$$

$$\frac{1}{-20} = \frac{1}{30} + \frac{1}{v}$$

$$\frac{1}{-20} = \frac{1}{30} + \frac{1}{v}$$

$$\frac{1}{v} = -\frac{1}{20} - \frac{1}{30} = -\frac{50}{600}$$

v = -12 cm

$$m = \frac{v}{u} = \frac{h_i}{h_o}$$

$$\frac{12}{30} = \frac{h_i}{4}$$

$h_i = 1.6\ cm$

79. An illuminated object 1.05 cm long is placed on and at right angles to the axis of a converging lens and an image 0.35 cm long is formed on a screen suitably placed at a distance of 80 cm from the object. Find the position of the lens and its focal length

$$\frac{v}{u} = \frac{h_i}{h_o}$$

$$\frac{v}{80} = \frac{0.35}{1.05}$$

v = 26.6 cm

$$\frac{1}{f} = \frac{1}{u} + \frac{1}{v}$$

$$\frac{1}{f} = \frac{1}{80} + \frac{1}{26.6}$$

f = 20 cm

80. A convex lens is used to project an image of a light source on to a screen. The screen is 30 cm from the light source, and the image is twice the size of the object. What focal length lens is required, and how far from the source must it be placed?

$$m = \frac{v}{u} = \frac{h_i}{h_o}$$

$$\frac{30}{u} = 3$$

u = 10 cm

$$\frac{1}{f} = \frac{1}{10} + \frac{1}{30} = \frac{40}{300}$$

f = 7.5 cm

81. An object 37.5 cm from a lens produces a real image 75.0 cm from the lens. What type of lens is it, and what is its focal length?

As the image is real image, the lens is convex lens.

$$\frac{1}{f} = \frac{1}{u} + \frac{1}{v}$$

$$\frac{1}{f} = \frac{1}{37.5} + \frac{1}{75} = \frac{75 + 37.5}{2812.5}$$

f = 25 cm

82.   The diagram represents the structure of the Earth.

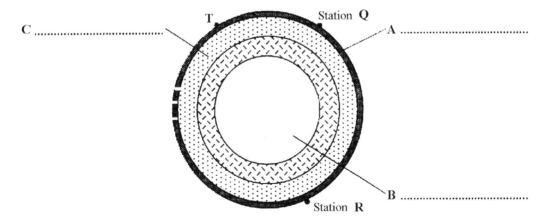

(a)   On the diagram, name the parts **A** to **C**.

   A is the crust, B inner core and C is mantle

(b)   An earthquake occurs at the point **T** on the Earth's surface.

Two types of shock wave are produced by the earthquake, P waves and S waves.

Describe **two** similarities and **two** differences between P waves and S waves as they travel through the Earth.

Similarities:

Both waves travel faster through denser materials, they can pass through solids.

Both waves can reflected, refracted and diffracted.

Differences:

P waves travels faster than S waves

only P waves pass through liquids

P longitudinal or S transverse

(c)   State whether P waves or S waves or both will reach:

(i)   Station Q;   P and S

(ii)   Station R.   P only

83.   (a)   All radio waves travel at 300 000 000 m/s in air.

(i)   Give the equation that links the frequency, speed and wavelength of a wave.

speed = frequency × wavelength

(ii)   Calculate the wavelength, in metres, of a radio wave which is broadcast at a frequency of 909 kHz. Show clearly how you work out your answer.

$$c = \lambda f$$

$$\lambda = \frac{c}{f} = \frac{300000000}{909000}$$

Wavelength = 330 m

(b)   The diagram shows what happens to the radio waves of part (a) as they approach and pass a hill.

(i)   What is the name given to the process which changes the shape of the waves?

Diffraction

(ii)   Explain why the person living in the house is unlikely to be able to receive television signals broadcast at a frequency of 550 000 kHz, even though they have the correct aerial.

The wavelength is too small compare with the size of the hill for diffraction to occur

(c)   Earthquakes produce longitudinal **P** and transverse **S** waves which travel through the Earth. These waves are recorded at earthquake stations around the world.

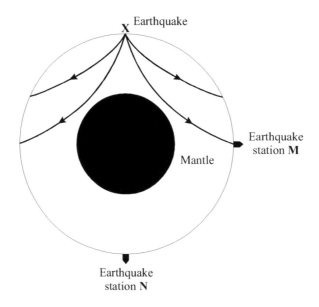

(i)   Why do **P** and **S** waves follow curved paths?

The density of rocks changes

(ii)   The diagram shows the seismic chart recorded at earthquake station **M** following an earthquake at **X**.

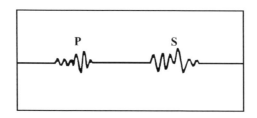

How would the seismic chart recorded at earthquake station **N** be different to that recorded at station **M**?

There will be no S waves at N station

Explain your answer.

As the outer core is liquid, S waves do not travel through a liquid

84. (a) A signal generator connected to a loudspeaker produces a sound wave. With the frequency of the signal generator set to 2000 Hz the sound wave has a wavelength of 0.17 m in air.

Calculate the speed of sound in air.

$$v = \lambda f = 0.17 \times 2000 = 340 \, m/s$$

(b) The speed of sound in water is 1400 m/s.

A sound wave has a frequency of 2000 Hz. Calculate its wavelength in water.

$$v = \lambda f$$

$$\lambda = \frac{v}{f} = \frac{1400}{2000} = 0.7 \, m$$

(c) Echo sounders are used at sea to locate underwater objects, such as submarines.
The diagram below shows how an echo sounder works.

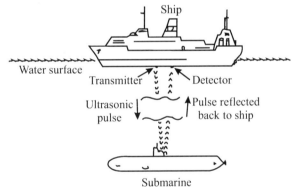

(i) What are ultrasonic waves?

Sound wave with a frequency higher than 20000 Hz

(ii) The pulse travels from the transmitter to the submarine and back to the detector. The time taken is 0.1 s.

Calculate the distance between the submarine and the ship.

$$v = \frac{d}{t}$$

$$d = v \times t = 1400 \times \frac{01}{2} = 70 \, m$$

(iii) State **one** other use for ultrasonic waves.

pre-natal scan

Cleaning teeth

Shatter kidney stones

85. The diagram shows the electromagnetic spectrum.

Gamma rays	X-rays	Ultra violet	Visible light	Infra red	Microwaves	Radio

(a) Name the type of electromagnetic radiation which is used:

(i) to prevent fresh food going bad quickly.   ....Gamma..............

(ii) to heat passengers' meals in an aeroplane....Infa red..or microwave.........

(b) (i) State **one** use of X-rays.

To produce an image of bones and teeth, airport security detection

(ii) State **one** use of ultra violet radiation.

Sunbed, detection of security markings, killing bacteria

(c) Longer wavelength radio waves are used for communications over very long distances without using satellites. Explain why this is possible.

Long Radio waves are reflected by ionosphere

86. (a) In the box are the names of five waves.

| infra red | microwaves | ultrasonic | ultraviolet | X-rays |

Which wave is used to:

(iv) send information to a satellite,

     microwaves

(v) (ii) toast bread

     Infra red

(vi) clean a valuable ring?

     Ultrasonic

(b) The diagram shows four oscilloscope wave traces. The controls of the oscilloscope were the same for each wave trace.

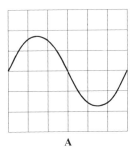

A

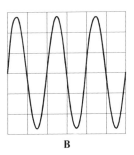

B

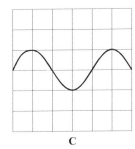

C

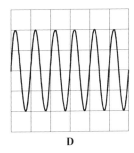

D

Which **one** of the waves traces, **A**, **B**, **C** or **D**, has:

(iii) the largest amplitude,

     B

(iv) the lowest frequency?

(v) ..A..

(c) The diagram shows a longitudinal wave in a stretched spring.

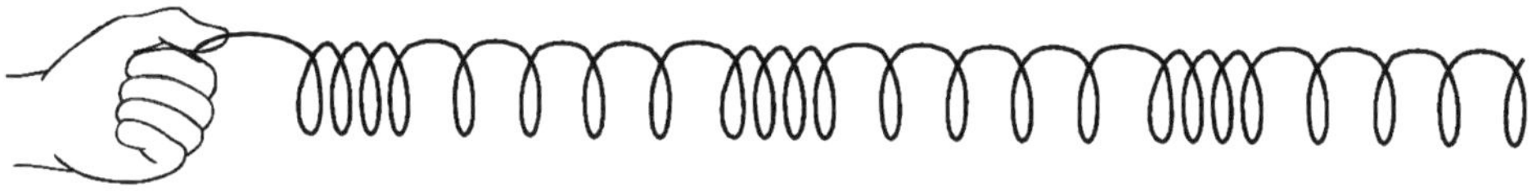

Disturbance   Direction of wave travel

Complete the sentence. You should put only **one** word in each space.

A longitudinal wave is one in which the …vibrations... causing the wave is in

the same......direction............. as that in which the wave moves.

(d) Which **one** of the following types of wave is longitudinal? Draw a ring around your answer.

light wave   sound wave   water wave

87. Explain how observations at the red end of the spectrum of light from galaxies have led to one theory about the origin of the Universe.

Light from distant galaxies shows a shift to the red end of spectrum. The wavelength increase can be explained by galaxies moving away from us; more distant galaxies have greater recession speed. Red shift can be observed in all directions, which suggests that universe is expanding

88. The Big Bang theory attempts to explain the origin of the Universe.

(i) What is the Universe?

all the galaxies

(i) What are the main ideas of the Big Bang theory?

At the big bang, all matter concentrated at a single point and the universe started to expand.

    (iii)   What is thought to be happening to the size of the Universe?

..........Expanding...............................

Manufactured by Amazon.ca
Bolton, ON